IRRESISTIBLE
DESSERTS

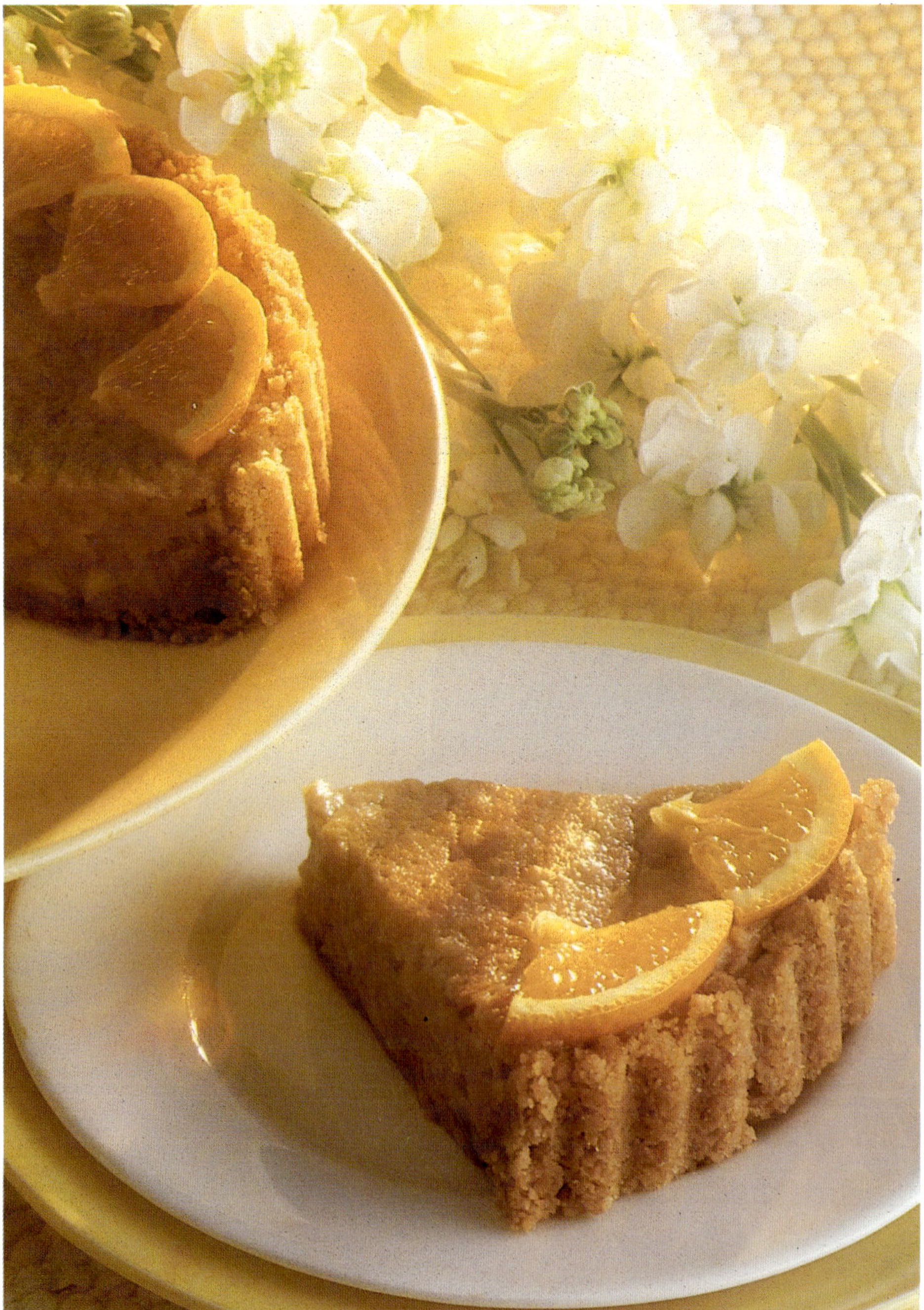

STEP-BY-STEP COOKING SERIES

IRRESISTIBLE DESSERTS

BARRON'S
Woodbury, New York · Toronto

First U.S. and Canadian edition published 1985 by
Barron's Educational Series, Inc.

Text copyright © 1984 by The National Magazine Company Limited.

Illustrations copyright © 1984 by The National Magazine Company Limited

The title of the British edition is *Desserts and Puddings*.

All rights reserved. No part of this book may be reproduced in any form,
by photostat, microfilm, xerography, or any other means, or incorporated
into any information retrieval system, electronic or mechanical, without the
written permission of the copyright owner.

All inquiries should be addressed to:

Barron's Educational Series, Inc.
113 Crossways Park Drive
Woodbury, New York 11797

International Standard Book No. 0-8120-5680-9

Library of Congress Catalog Card No. 85-11125

Library of Congress Cataloging-in-Publication Data
Main entry under title:

Irresistible Desserts.

    (Step-by-step cooking series)
    Includes index.
    Originally published as: Desserts and Puddings, 1984.
    1. Desserts. I. Series.
TX773.I77 1985 641.8'6 85-11125
ISBN 0-8120-5680-9

Printed in Italy

5 6 7 8   9 8 7 6 5 4 3 2 1

Contents

Introduction	7
Pies and Pastries	8
Dinner Party Desserts	26
Traditional and Everyday Desserts	58
Custards, Soufflés and Creams	84
Fruit Desserts	106

Useful Information and Basic Recipes

Basic Equipment	130
Cooking with Fruits and Nuts	132
Cooking with Chocolate and Cream	143
Cooking with Eggs	145
Pastry Making	149
Sweet Sauces, Butters, Sugar and Gelatin	153
Index	159

COOKING NOTES

KITCHEN TIPS

All spoon measures are level unless otherwise stated. All fruits and vegetables are medium size, unless indicated.

- Large eggs should be used, except when otherwise stated.
- Granulated sugar is used, unless otherwise indicated.
- Flour is all-purpose, pre-sifted, unless otherwise mentioned.

Some recipes call for self-rising flour. This flour is available in all supermarkets, but if desired, for each cup of self-rising flour you can substitute 1 cup of all-purpose flour and 1 teaspoon baking soda.

> All recipes in this book serve SIX PEOPLE unless otherwise indicated.

FOR CANADIAN COOKS

The ingredients in this book are given for U.S. customary measuring units. Cooks in Canada must consider the differing types of flour available to them and adjust cake recipes accordingly. Use the following measurements as a general guide:

1 U.S. cup = 236 mL or 8 fluid ounces
1 Canadian cup = 250 mL
1 tablespoon butter = 15 g or $\frac{1}{2}$ ounce
1 cup butter = 225 g or 8 ounces
1 cup all-purpose flour = 150 g or 5 ounces
1 cup granulated sugar = 190 g or $6\frac{1}{2}$ ounces
1 cup confectioners sugar = 80 g or $2\frac{2}{3}$ ounces

KEY TO SYMBOLS

$\boxed{1.00*}$ Indicates minimum preparation and cooking times in hours and minutes. They do not include prepared items in the list of ingredients; calculated times apply only to the method. An asterisk * indicates extra time should be allowed, so check the note below symbols.

🎩 Chef's hats indicate degree of difficulty of a recipe: no hat means it is straightforward; one hat slightly more complicated; two hats indicates that it is for more advanced cooks.

$ Indicates a recipe which is good value for money; $ $ indicates an expensive recipe. No $ sign indicates an inexpensive recipe.

✱ Indicates that a recipe will freeze. If there is no symbol, the recipe is unsuitable for freezing. An asterisk * indicates special freezer instructions, so check the note immediately below the symbols.

$\boxed{309\text{ cals}}$ Indicates calories per serving, including any serving suggestions (for example, cream, to serve) given in the list of ingredients.

INTRODUCTION

Stuck for ideas when it comes to the dessert course? Look no further than this book—from everyday puddings to wonderful dinner party desserts, it's literally packed full of new and exciting ideas, each recipe with its own fabulous full-color photograph for you to feast your eyes on as well as your taste buds!

From the five separate chapters of recipes, you can choose a dessert to suit any occasion, and there are step-by-step illustrations for problem-free preparation. Pies and Pastries includes recipes from all over the world; Dinner Party Desserts gives you lots of spectacular ideas, all easy to follow and many cook-ahead; Traditional and Everyday goes back to basics with all-time favorites; and Custards et al. has lots of luscious desserts from two of the simplest of ingredients. To round off the recipe section, there is Fruit Desserts, fresh and simple dishes which make the most of seasonal fruits.

At the back of the book there is a special section of Useful Information and Basic Recipes. Here you will find everything you need to help you when making desserts—advice on the best equipment to buy and use, information on ingredients—fruits, nuts, sugar, gelatine, chocolate, cream and eggs—plus tips on making pastry, meringues, crêpes and soufflés. And a selection of useful basic recipes which you'll find yourself turning to again and again.

IRRESISTIBLE DESSERTS

Pies and Pastries

Crisp, light pastry with sweet and tasty fillings make marvelous family and dinner party desserts. And they have the added benefit of making a small amount of fruit go a long way—ideal for feeding a large gathering. Serve these pies and pastries with a perfectly smooth homemade custard sauce, or be wickedly extravagant and top with lashings of fresh whipped cream.

OLD-FASHIONED APPLE PIE

1.10 | $ | ✱ | 651 cals

shortcrust pastry (see page 152) for a 9-inch pan
1½ lb cooking apples
finely grated rind and juice of ½ a lemon
⅓ cup sugar
⅓ cup dark brown sugar
1 Tbsp all-purpose flour
pinch of grated nutmeg
¼ tsp ground cinnamon
finely grated rind and juice of ½ an orange
⅓ cup light raisins
1–2 Tbsp butter or margarine
sugar, to dredge
custard sauce or light cream, to serve

1 Roll out two thirds of the pastry on a floured work surface and use to line a 9-inch pie pan. Refrigerate for 30 minutes with the remaining dough wrapped in plastic wrap.

2 Meanwhile, peel and core the apples, then slice them thickly into a bowl of cold water to which the lemon juice has been added.

3 Mix the sugars, flour, nutmeg, cinnamon, lemon and orange rinds together and sprinkle a little of this on to the pastry lining.

4 Cover the bottom of the pastry lining with half of the sliced apples, then sprinkle with half the raisins and half of the remaining sugar mixture. Repeat, using all the apples, raisins and sugar.

5 Sprinkle the fruit with the orange juice and dot with butter or margarine.

6 Roll out the remaining pastry and use to cover the pie, sealing the edges well. Slash the top twice to let steam escape.

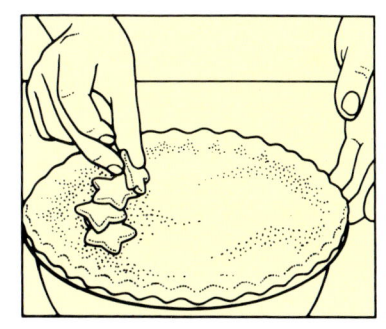

7 Use the pastry trimmings to make decorations for the pie. Brush the top of the pie with water and place on the decorations. Dredge with sugar.

8 Bake in the oven at 375°F for 35–40 minutes until the fruit is tender and the top is golden brown. Serve warm, with custard sauce or cream.

OLD-FASHIONED APPLE PIE

Cinnamon is always one of the favorite spices to use with apples, so too are nutmeg and ginger.
  To give your apple pies a real old-fashioned flavor, add one or two quinces instead of some of the apples.

IRRESISTIBLE DESSERTS

Peach Pie

| 1.25* | $ | 555 cals |

* plus 15 minutes cooling
1½ cups all-purpose flour
½ cup finely chopped walnuts
½ cup softened butter or margarine, cut into pieces
½ cup sugar
2 egg yolks
2 Tbsp water
6 large peaches, about 2 lb
1 egg white and sugar, to glaze
light cream, to serve

1 Place the flour on a clean, dry work surface and sprinkle the chopped walnuts over the top. Make a well in the center, then place the butter in it with the sugar, egg yolks and water.

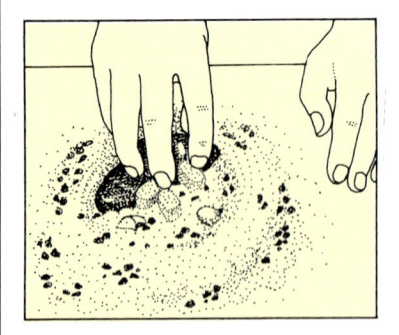

2 With the fingertips of one hand only, pinch the well ingredients together until evenly blended. Using a palette knife, cut the flour into the well ingredients and then knead the dough lightly until just smooth.

3 Roll out two thirds on a floured work surface and use to line a 9-inch loose-bottomed fluted tart pan. Refrigerate for 30 minutes.

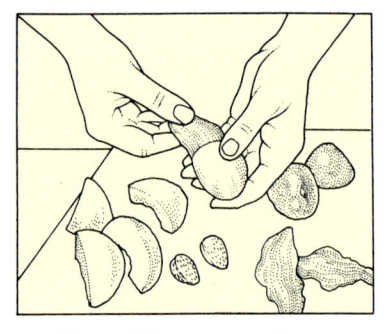

4 Meanwhile, quarter the peaches and ease away from the stone. Peel off the skins carefully and divide each quarter in two lengthways.

5 Arrange the peaches in the tart pan. Roll out the remaining pastry and use to cover the pie, sealing the edges well. Make a small hole in the center to let steam escape.

6 Bake in the oven, on a preheated baking sheet, at 400°F for about 20–25 minutes or until it is just beginning to brown.

7 Brush the top of the pie with lightly beaten egg white and dust with sugar. Return to the oven for a further 10 minutes or until well browned and crisp. Cool for 15 minutes in the pan before removing. Serve while still slightly warm, with cream.

Pumpkin Pie

| 1.25 | $ | 670 cals |

Serves 4

shortcrust pastry (see page 152) for a 9-inch pie
1 lb pumpkin
2 eggs
$\frac{2}{3}$ cup sugar
$\frac{1}{4}$ cup milk
pinch of grated nutmeg
pinch of ground ginger
2 tsp ground cinnamon
whipped cream, to serve

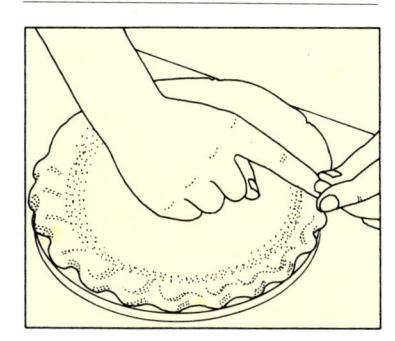

1 Roll out the pastry on a floured work surface and use to line a 9-inch fluted tart pan or pie pan; trim and decorate the edges. Refrigerate for about 30 minutes.

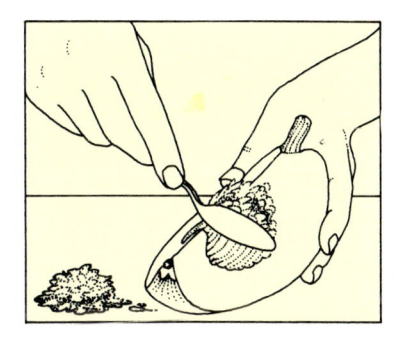

2 Meanwhile, cut the pumpkin into pieces, remove any seeds and cut off the outside skin.

3 Steam the pieces of pumpkin between two plates over a pan of boiling water for 15–20 minutes until tender. Drain thoroughly, then mash well with a fork or purée in an electric blender or food processor.

4 Beat the eggs with the sugar. Add the pumpkin purée, the milk and spices. Blend well and pour into the pastry.

5 Bake in the oven at 425°F for 15 minutes, then reduce the temperature to 350°F and bake for a further 30 minutes or until the filling is set. Serve warm, with whipped cream.

IRRESISTIBLE DESSERTS

Mincemeat Meringue Tartlets

| 1.00 | 🍳 | $ | ✱ | 165 cals |

Makes 12

shortcrust pastry (see page 152)
2 egg whites
$\frac{2}{3}$ cup sugar
1 medium cooking apple
$\frac{1}{4}$ cup mincemeat
2 Tbsp orange-flavored liqueur or brandy
finely grated rind of 1 orange

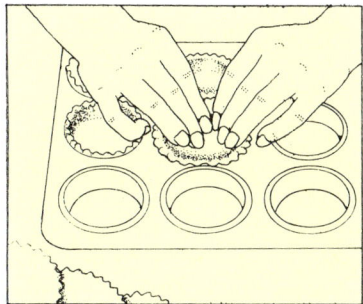

1 Roll out the pastry thinly on a floured work surface, then cut out twelve 3-inch rounds using a fluted pastry cutter. Use to line twelve muffin cups. Brush the rounds with a little egg white. Refrigerate for 30 minutes. Prick the bases and bake in the oven at 400°F for 10–15 minutes until set.

2 Meanwhile, whisk the remaining egg whites in a clean, dry bowl until stiff, then beat in 1 Tbsp of the sugar. Continue whisking until the meringue stands in stiff peaks, then fold in the rest of the sugar, reserving 2 tsp.

3 Peel and core the apple, then grate into a bowl. Mix in the mincemeat, liqueur and rind.

4 Spoon the mincemeat mixture into the tarts, dividing it equally between them.

5 Top with the meringue, either by piping it with a large star nozzle or by spooning it on. Make sure there are no gaps between meringue and pastry. Sprinkle with the reserved sugar.

6 Bake in the oven at 375°F for 15–20 minutes until the meringue is crisp and golden. Serve the tarts warm or cold.

MINCEMEAT MERINGUE TARTLETS

Topping mincemeat tarts with meringue instead of the usual pastry makes them somehow look more festive (especially if you pipe the meringue on) and of course makes them much lighter to eat. The orange-flavored liqueur or brandy in the recipe can be omitted, but try to use a good-quality mincemeat — brands containing alcohol are the nicest.

IRRESISTIBLE DESSERTS

Strawberry Custard Tart

| 0.35* | 🕐 | $ $ | 455–556 cals |

* plus 1 hour 10 minutes cooling and about 1½ hours chilling

Serves 6–8

1¼ cups all-purpose flour
3 Tbsp plus ½ cup sugar
½ cup butter or margarine
3 eggs
2 Tbsp cornstarch
2 cups milk
few drops of vanilla extract
12 oz strawberries, hulled
light cream, to serve

1 Mix the flour with 3 Tbsp sugar in a bowl, then cut in the butter until the mixture resembles fine cornmeal. Form into a soft dough with 1 egg. Knead lightly on a floured work surface until just smooth.

2 Roll out the pastry on a floured work surface and use to line a 9-inch fluted tart dish. Refrigerate for 30 minutes. Prick the pastry and bake in the oven at 400°F for 20 minutes or until pale golden and cooked through. Cool in the dish for 30–40 minutes.

3 Mix the cornstarch to a smooth paste with a little of the milk. Separate the remaining eggs and mix the egg yolks with the cornstarch paste. Put the rest of the milk in a saucepan with the remaining sugar and the vanilla extract. Bring to the boil, then remove from the heat and pour in the cornstarch mixture. Return to the boil, stirring, and boil for 2 minutes until thickened. Cover with plastic wrap and cool for 30 minutes. (Whisk if necessary to remove lumps.)

4 Thinly slice the strawberries into the cooked pastry, reserving a few for decoration. Whisk the egg whites until stiff and fold into the cold custard mixture. Smooth the custard mixture evenly over the strawberries. Refrigerate for 1 hour until set.

5 Serve the tart decorated with the reserved strawberry slices, preferably within 2 hours of completion. Serve with cream.

Walnut Meringue Tart

|0.55*| $ |475–658 cals|

* plus 30 minutes chilling and 1 hour cooling

Serves 4–6

$\frac{1}{4}$ cup butter or margarine
2 Tbsp plus 1 cup light brown sugar
1 egg yolk
$\frac{3}{4}$ cup all-purpose flour
2 egg whites
$\frac{1}{2}$ tsp vanilla extract
1 cup walnuts, chopped
whipped cream, to serve

1 Melt the butter, cool for 5 minutes, then stir in 2 Tbsp of the sugar with the egg yolk and flour. Knead lightly, then press over the base and up the sides of a greased 9-inch pie plate. Refrigerate for 30 minutes.

2 Whisk the egg whites in a clean, dry bowl until stiff, but not dry. Gradually whisk in the remaining sugar, keeping mixture stiff. Add the vanilla extract with the last spoonful of sugar.

3 Fold in the chopped walnuts, then spoon into the pastry-lined pie plate.

4 Bake in the oven at 350°F for 30 minutes until the filling is well risen. Cool completely for 1 hour. As the meringue cools it will shrink and crack slightly.

5 Serve the walnut tart cold, cut in wedges, with whipped cream over the top.

Tarte Française

1.50* ⏲ ❄ 657 cals

* plus 30 minutes chilling and 10 minutes cooling

$1\frac{1}{4}$ cups all-purpose flour
pinch of salt
$\frac{3}{4}$ cup butter or margarine
7 tsp sugar
1 egg yolk
3 Tbsp water
2 lb cooking apples
$\frac{1}{2}$ cup apricot jam
$\frac{1}{3}$ cup sugar
finely grated rind of $\frac{1}{2}$ a lemon
2 Tbsp apple brandy or brandy
$\frac{1}{2}$ lb eating apples
2 Tbsp lemon juice

1 Put the flour and salt in a bowl. Rub in $\frac{1}{2}$ cup of the butter until the mixture resembles fine cornmeal; stir in 6 tsp of the sugar. Mix the egg yolk with 1 Tbsp of the water and stir into the pastry mixture. Knead lightly on a floured work surface until just smooth.

2 Roll out the pastry and use to line a 8-inch fluted tart pan. Refrigerate for 30 minutes.

3 Prick the base of the tart and bake in the oven at 350°F for 15–20 minutes until just set.

4 Cut the cooking apples into quarters; core and roughly chop. Melt the remaining $\frac{1}{4}$ cup butter in a saucepan and add the apples with the remaining water. Cover the pan tightly and cook gently for about 15 minutes until soft and mushy.

5 Rub the apples through a sieve into a large clean pan. Add half the apricot jam with $\frac{1}{3}$ cup sugar, lemon rind and apple brandy. Cook over high heat for about 15 minutes stirring all the time until all excess liquid has evaporated and the mixture is well reduced and thickened.

6 Spoon the thick apple purée into the pastry and smooth the surface. Peel, quarter, core and slice the eating apples very thinly. Arrange in an overlapping circle around the edge of the tart. Brush lightly with lemon juice; sprinkle with the remaining sugar.

7 Return the tart to the oven and bake for a further 25–30 minutes or until the pastry and apples are lightly colored. Cool for 10 minutes.

8 Gently warm the remaining jam with 1 Tbsp lemon juice and, when well blended, sieve into a small bowl. While still warm, brush carefully over the top of the tart until evenly glazed. Serve warm or chilled.

PIES AND PASTRIES

IRRESISTIBLE DESSERTS

Pears en Chemise

1.00* $ $ 638 cals

* plus 30 minutes chilling

Serves 4

| 13-oz package frozen puff pastry, thawed |
| 4 large dessert pears (Comice or D'Anjou) |
| finely grated rind and juice of 1 lemon |
| 9 tsp red currant jelly |
| 1 egg, beaten, to glaze |
| 2 tsp sugar |
| cream, to serve |

1 Cut the pastry into four and roll out each piece on a lightly floured work surface to a 7-inch square.

2 Peel the pears and core them carefully from the bottom. Leave the stalks on. Brush them immediately with lemon juice to prevent discoloration.

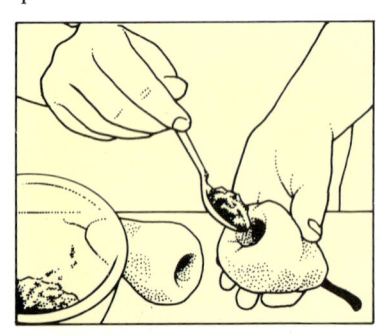

3 Mix together the lemon rind and half the red currant jelly. Put 1 tsp into the cavity of each pear, then stand the pears upright in the center of each pastry square. Brush the edge of the pastry with water.

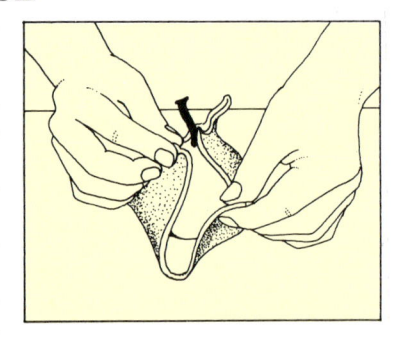

4 Bring the four corners of each square to the top of each pear and press the edges to seal.

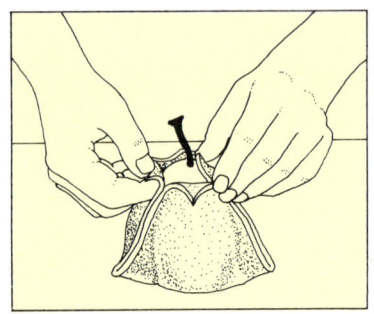

5 Fold back the four points to expose the stalk and allow steam to escape. Stand the pears on a dampened baking sheet and refrigerate for 30 minutes.

6 Brush the pears all over with beaten egg and sprinkle with the sugar. Bake in the oven at 425°F for 15–20 minutes until the pastry is crisp and golden.

7 Warm the remaining red currant jelly and brush all over the pastry. Serve warm, with cream.

PIES AND PASTRIES

IRRESISTIBLE DESSERTS

BUTTERSCOTCH CREAM PIE

1.15* $ $ ✱ 574 cals

* plus 30 minutes chilling and 1 hour cooling

| 1¼ cups all-purpose flour |
| ¼ tsp salt |
| ½ cup plus 3 Tbsp butter or margarine |
| 2 tsp sugar |
| 5 egg yolks and 1 egg white |
| ⅔ cup milk |
| ¾ cup evaporated milk |
| ⅓ cup dark brown sugar |
| 1 Tbsp cornstarch |
| 2 cups whipped cream |

1 Put the flour into a bowl with half the salt. Add the ½ cup butter in pieces and rub in with the fingertips until the mixture resembles fine cornmeal.

2 Stir in the sugar and 1 egg yolk and draw the dough together to form a ball. Add a few drops of cold water if the dough is too dry.

3 Press the dough gently into a 8-inch loose-bottomed fluted tart pan. Refrigerate for 30 minutes.

4 Prick the base of the pastry and bake in the oven at 400°F for 10 minutes. Brush the pastry with the egg white, then return to the oven and bake for a further 10 minutes until crisp and lightly colored. Leave to cool.

5 Meanwhile, make the filling. Put the milk and evaporated milk in a saucepan and scald by bringing up to boiling point. Put the brown sugar, cornstarch, remaining butter, egg yolks and salt in a heavy-based saucepan. Heat gently until the butter has melted and sugar dissolved, then gradually stir in the scalded milks. Stir well until heated through.

6 Cook over gentle heat, whisking constantly until the custard is thick. (Don't worry if the mixture is lumpy at first—keep whisking vigorously with a balloon whisk and it will become smooth.)

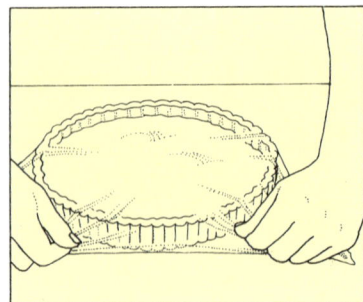

7 Remove from the heat and cool slightly, then pour into the baked tart shell. Cover the surface of the butterscotch cream closely with plastic wrap (to prevent a skin forming) and leave for about 1 hour until completely cold.

8 Serve with whipped cream. Chill until serving time.

PIES AND PASTRIES

IRRESISTIBLE DESSERTS

CHERRY STRUDEL

3.00 $ $ ✱
523–784 cals

Serves 4–6

| 1½ cups plus 1–2 Tbsp all-purpose flour |
| ½ tsp salt |
| 1 egg, lightly beaten |
| 2 Tbsp vegetable oil |
| 4 Tbsp lukewarm water |
| 1½ lb ripe black cherries, pitted and very finely chopped |
| 3 Tbsp black cherry jam |
| 2 Tbsp kirsch |
| ½ cup sugar |
| ½ tsp ground cinnamon |
| 3 Tbsp butter, melted |
| 1 cup ground almonds |
| confectioners sugar |

1 Put 1½ cups flour and salt into a large mixing bowl, make a well in the center and pour in the egg and oil. Add the water gradually, stirring with a fork to make a soft, sticky dough.

2 Work the dough in the bowl until it leaves the sides, turn it out on to a lightly floured surface and knead for 15 minutes. Form into a ball, place on a cloth and cover with a warmed bowl. Leave the dough to rest in a warm place for about 1 hour.

3 In a bowl, thoroughly mix together the cherries, the cherry jam, the kirsch, sugar and ground cinnamon.

4 Warm a rolling pin. Spread a clean cotton cloth on the table and sprinkle lightly with 1–2 Tbsp flour. Place the dough on the cloth and roll out into a rectangle about ⅛ inch thick, lifting and turning it to prevent it sticking to the cloth.

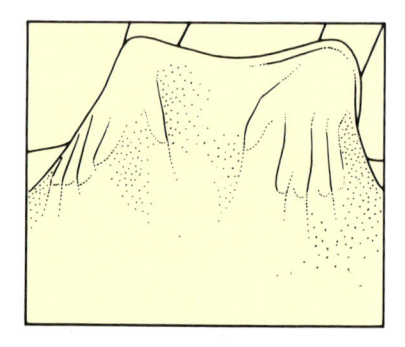

5 Gently stretch the dough, working from the center to the outside and using the backs of the hands until it is paper-thin. Trim the edges to form a rectangle about 27 × 24 inches. Leave the strudel dough on the cloth to dry and rest for about 15 minutes before filling and rolling.

PIES AND PASTRIES

6 Position the dough with one of the long sides towards you, brush with half the melted butter and sprinkle with ground almonds. Spread the cherry mixture over the dough, leaving a 2-inch border uncovered all round the edge.

MAKING STRUDEL DOUGH

Elasticity is the key word when it comes to making strudel pastry.

Strudel dough is unique in that it is exceptionally strong; it is not difficult to make as long as the instructions given in the method are followed. The 15-minute kneading in step 2 is vitally important to develop the gluten in the flour and so make the dough elastic and strong enough to be rolled so thin.

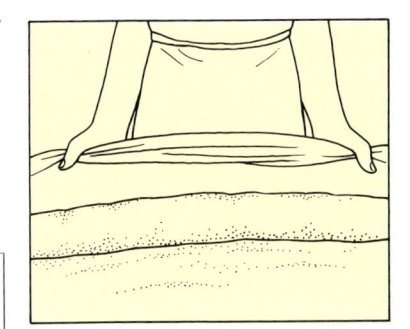

7 Fold the pastry edges over the cherry mixture, toward the center. Lift the corners of the cloth nearest to you over the pastry, causing the strudel to roll up, but stop after each turn in order to pat into shape and to keep the roll even.

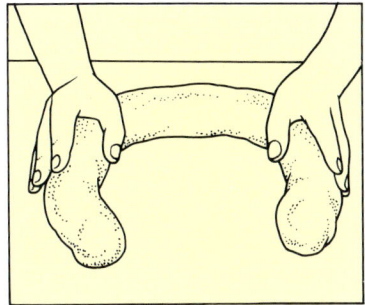

8 Form the roll into a horseshoe shape, brush it with the rest of the melted butter and slide it on to a buttered baking sheet. Bake in the oven at 375°F for about 40 minutes or until golden brown. Sift the strudel lightly with confectioners sugar. Serve warm cut into 4–6 slices.

Fudge Nut Pie

| 1.35 | $ $ ✱ | 607 cals* |

* excluding ice cream; 702 cals with $\frac{1}{4}$ cup ice cream

Serves 8

| shortcrust pastry (see page 152) for a 9-inch fluted tart pan |
| 2 oz semisweet chocolate, broken into pieces |
| $\frac{1}{4}$ cup butter or margarine |
| $1\frac{1}{3}$ cups sugar |
| $\frac{1}{2}$ cup light brown sugar |
| $\frac{1}{2}$ cup milk |
| 3 Tbsp corn syrup |
| 1 tsp vanilla extract |
| $\frac{1}{4}$ tsp salt |
| 3 eggs |
| 1 cup chopped mixed nuts |
| confectioners sugar, to decorate |
| vanilla ice cream, to serve |

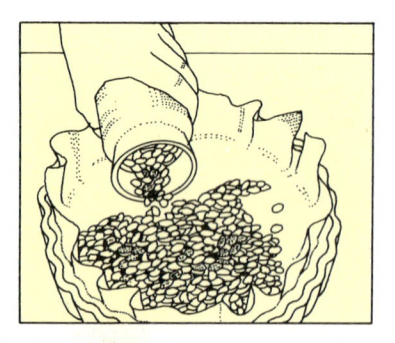

1 Roll out the pastry on a floured work surface and use to line a 9-inch fluted tart pan. Bake in the oven at 400°F for 10–15 minutes until set. Set aside to cool.

2 While the pastry is cooling, put the chocolate and butter in a large heatproof bowl standing over a pan of simmering water. Heat gently until melted.

3 Remove bowl from the pan and add the remaining ingredients, except for the chopped nuts. Beat with a wooden spoon until well mixed, then stir in the nuts.

4 Pour the filling into the pastry and bake in the oven at 350°F for 45–60 minutes or until puffy and golden. Sift lightly with confectioners sugar. Serve hot or cold with ice cream.

PIES AND PASTRIES

IRRESISTIBLE DESSERTS

Dinner Party Desserts

A dinner party is the one occasion when you can really go to town with the dessert course. Show off your culinary skills and create something really special which is sure to impress your guests. Chocolate, cream, liqueur, fresh fruit, meringue and ice cream can all be used with abandon—and they're all here in this chapter to tempt your tastebuds.

DINNER PARTY DESSERTS

CRÊPES SUZETTE

| 0.40* | 🍳 | $ $ | ✱* | 370–554 cals |

*not including making the crêpe batter; freeze cooked crêpes only
Serves 4–6

7 Tbsp orange-flavored liqueur
crêpe batter made with $1\frac{1}{4}$ cups milk (see page 148)
$\frac{1}{2}$ cup unsalted butter
$\frac{2}{3}$ cup sugar
finely grated rind and juice of 1 large orange

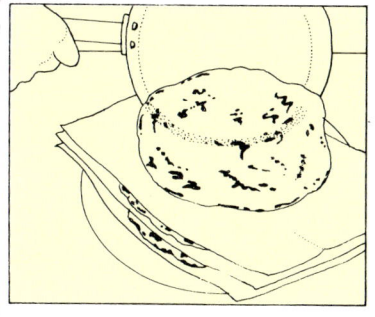

1 Stir 1 Tbsp liqueur into the batter, then make 8–12 crêpes in the usual way (see page 148). Slide each crêpe out of the pan on to a warm plate and stack with wax paper in between.

2 To serve, heat the butter and sugar together in a large, heavy-based frying pan until thick and syrupy. Add 2 Tbsp liqueur and the orange rind and juice and heat through.

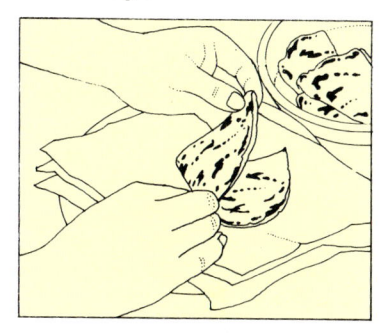

3 Fold the crêpes into triangle shapes by folding each one in half, then in half again. Place them in the frying pan and spoon over the sauce so that they become evenly coated.

4 Heat the remaining liqueur gently in a ladle or separate small pan. Transfer the crêpes and sauce to a warmed serving dish, pour over the warmed liqueur and set alight. Carry the crêpes to the table immediately, while they are still flaming.

CRÊPES SUZETTE

A classic French dessert; with its spectacular flambéed finish, crêpes Suzette is just perfect for a special dinner party. Traditionally flambéed at the table in a copper chafing dish in restaurants specialising in *haute cuisine*, the crêpes can look just as good at home carried flaming to the table on a silver or fine china plate.

This recipe uses orange juice and orange-flavored liqueur, although the original classic recipe contained mandarin orange juice and orange liqueur, both in the crêpe batter and in the filling. If you wish to make this classic version rather than our more modern variation, try the following: Add 1 tsp each mandarin orange juice and orange-flavored liqueur to the crêpe batter before frying. Make a filling by creaming together $\frac{1}{4}$ cup of unsalted butter and $\frac{1}{3}$ cup sugar. Work in the finely grated rind and juice of 1 mandarin orange and 1 Tbsp orange-flavored liqueur. When the crêpes are cooked, spread them with filling, fold into triangles, place in the serving dish and flambé with more liqueur.

Baked Alaska

0.30* | $ | 245–326 cals

*plus 2 hours macerating

Serves 6–8

½ lb fresh or frozen raspberries
2 Tbsp orange-flavored liqueur
8-inch cooked sponge shell (see page 152)
4 eggs whites, at room temperature
1⅓ cups sugar
1 pint block vanilla ice cream

1 Place the fresh or frozen raspberries on a shallow dish and sprinkle over the liqueur. Cover and leave to macerate for 2 hours, turning occasionally.

2 Place the sponge shell on a large ovenproof serving dish and spoon the raspberries and juice into the center.

3 Whisk the 4 egg whites in a clean, dry bowl until stiff, but not dry. Add 4 tsp sugar and whisk again, keeping the mixture stiff. Sprinkle over the remaining sugar and fold through gently.

4 Fit a pastry bag with a large star nozzle and fill with the meringue mixture.

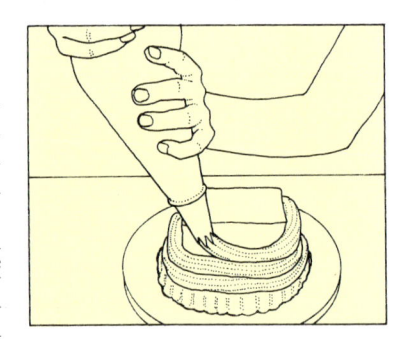

5 Place the block of ice cream on top of the raspberries, then immediately pipe the meringue on top. Start from the sponge base and pipe the meringue around and over the ice cream until it is completely covered, leaving no gaps.

6 Immediately place the completed Alaska in a preheated oven and bake at 450°F for 3–4 minutes. At this stage the meringue should be nicely tinged with brown. Watch the meringue carefully as it burns easily. Do not overcook or the ice cream will become too soft. Serve at once, before the ice cream begins to melt.

BAKED ALASKA

A spectacular dessert for a special dinner party, the recipe for baked Alaska originated in the U.S., where it is also sometimes called Norwegian Omelet or *omelette norvégienne* in French. Although impressive to serve, Baked Alaska is in fact surprisingly easy to make; the essential thing is to allow yourself unhurried time in the kitchen before serving—Baked Alaska cannot be kept waiting once it is cooked!

To help things run smoothly, prepare as much as you can before your dinner party starts. Make the sponge shell and top with the fruit up to the end of stage 2, then whisk the meringue until stiff as in stage 3. Once your guests have finished their main course, you will only have to pop the ice cream on top of the fruit, pipe over the meringue and bake the dessert in the oven for a few minutes.

DINNER PARTY DESSERTS

IRRESISTIBLE DESSERTS

DINNER PARTY DESSERTS

PETITS POTS AU CHOCOLAT

| 1.45* | $ | 410 cals |

* plus 1 hour cooling
1 Tbsp coffee beans
3 egg yolks
1 egg
½ cup sugar
3 cups half and half
3 oz semisweet chocolate
⅔ cup whipping cream and chocolate coffee beans, to decorate

1 Toast the coffee beans under a broiler for a few minutes, then set aside.

2 Beat together the egg yolks, whole egg and sugar until the mixture is very pale.

3 Place the half and half and coffee beans in a saucepan and bring to the boil.

4 Strain the half and half on to the egg mixture, stirring all the time. Discard the coffee beans.

5 Return the mixture to the saucepan, break up the chocolate and add to the pan. Stir over gentle heat (do not boil) for about 5 minutes until the chocolate has almost melted and mixture is *slightly* thickened. Whisk lightly until evenly blended.

6 Stand six individual ⅔ cup ramekin dishes or custard pots in a roasting pan, then pour in enough hot water to come halfway up the sides of the dishes. Pour the custard mixture slowly into the dishes, dividing it equally between them. Cover, then bake in the oven at 300°F for 1–1¼ hours or until the custard is lightly set.

7 Leave to cool. To serve, whip the cream and spoon into a pastry bag fitted with a large star nozzle. Pipe a whirl on top and decorate with coffee beans.

CHOCOLATE

These little chocolate pots rely heavily on the flavor of the chocolate used in their making. So it is essential to use a good-quality chocolate. Semisweet chocolate is specified because it has better melting qualities than milk chocolate, and it also contains less sugar. Look for Swiss and other European chocolates, such as Lindt.

31

IRRESISTIBLE DESSERTS

Nègre en Chemise

| 0.30* | 🍴 | $ $ | ❄ | 854 cals |

* plus 2–3 hours setting

Serves 8

| 12 oz semisweet chocolate, broken into pieces |
| $\frac{1}{2}$ cup water |
| $\frac{1}{3}$ cup butter or margarine |
| $\frac{1}{2}$ cup praline, crushed (see page 142) |
| 1 Tbsp brandy |
| 2 cups whipping cream |
| chocolate circles, to decorate (see page 144) |

1 Put the chocolate and water in a heatproof bowl standing over a pan of simmering water. Heat gently until melted. Remove bowl from the pan and cool slightly.

2 Meanwhile, cream the butter in a bowl. Add the melted chocolate and gradually beat in praline. Stir in brandy.

3 Lightly whip the cream and fold half into the chocolate mixture. Turn the mixture into a lightly oiled 6-cups mold and refrigerate for 2–3 hours until set.

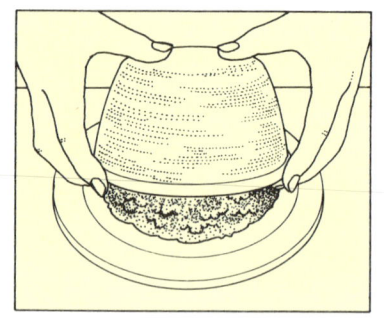

4 To serve. Quickly dip the mold into hot water, place a serving plate on top and invert. Lift off the mold.

5 Fill a pastry bag, fitted with a large star nozzle, with the remaining cream and pipe around the base of the dessert. Decorate with chocolate circles. Refrigerate until serving time.

DINNER PARTY DESSERTS

CHILLED ZABAGLIONE

| 0.25* | 🎩 | $ | 366 cals |

* plus 30 minutes cooling and 2 hours freezing

4 egg yolks
$\frac{2}{3}$ sugar
$\frac{1}{2}$ cup marsala
1 cup whipping cream
2 Tbsp confectioners sugar
orange shreds, to decorate
ladyfingers, to serve

1. Put the egg yolks and sugar in a large bowl. Beat together, add the marsala and beat again.

2. Place the bowl over a saucepan of simmering water and heat gently, whisking the mixture until it is very thick and creamy and forms soft peaks. Remove the bowl from the heat and leave to cool for about 30 minutes.

3. Place the cream in a bowl and sift in the confectioners sugar. Whisk until stiff then fold into the cooled egg mixture. Chill in the refrigerator for about 2 hours until firm.

4. Spoon the iced zabaglione into six individual glasses, decorate with orange shreds and serve with ladyfingers.

IRRESISTIBLE DESSERTS

Snowcap Iced Pudding

| 1.15* | $ $ | ❄ | 303–405 cals |

* plus 2 hours setting and overnight freezing

Serves 6–8

2/3 cup kirsch
4 Tbsp water
about 15 ladyfingers
2 cups chocolate chip ice cream
1/2 lb ripe cherries, pitted and roughly chopped
2 cups vanilla ice cream
2/3 cup whipping cream

1 Cut out a circle of wax paper and use it to line the base of a 1 1/2-quart pudding mold.

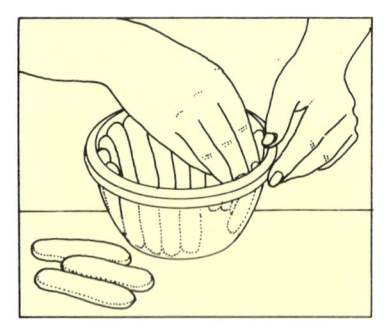

2 Mix the kirsch with the water and dip the ladyfingers one at a time into the mixture. Use to line the sides of the pudding mold, trimming them to fit so that there are no gaps in between. Fill the base of the mold with leftover pieces of sponge. Refrigerate for 15 minutes.

3 Stir any remaining kirsch liquid into the chocolate ice cream and mash the ice cream well with a fork to soften it slightly and make it smooth.

4 Spoon the chocolate ice cream into the mold and work it up the sides of the ladyfingers to the top of the mold so that it forms an even layer. Freeze for about 2 hours until firm.

5 Mix the cherries into the vanilla ice cream and mash well with a fork as in step 3.

6 Spoon the vanilla ice cream into the center of the mold and smooth it over the top so that it covers the chocolate ice cream and the ladyfingers. Cover with foil and freeze overnight.

7 To serve, whip the cream until it will just hold its shape. Run a knife around the inside of the mold, then turn the ice cream out on to a serving plate.

8 Spoon the cream over the top and let it just start to run down the sides, then freeze immediately for about 15 minutes or until the cream has frozen solid. Serve straight from the freezer.

DINNER PARTY DESSERTS

IRRESISTIBLE DESSERTS

DINNER PARTY DESSERTS

CHARLOTTE RUSSE

1.35* | $ | 447 cals

* plus 50 minutes cooling and 4 hours setting

| 3-oz package lemon Jello |
| 2 cups boiling water |
| 3 Tbsp lemon juice |
| 2 glacé cherries, quartered |
| piece of angelica, cut into triangles |
| 1⅓ cups milk |
| 1 vanilla bean |
| 3 Tbsp water |
| 3 tsp gelatine |
| 3 egg yolks |
| 3 Tbsp sugar |
| about 18 ladyfingers |
| 1⅓ cups whipping cream |

1 Dissolve the Jello in a bowl, according to the package instructions, using the lemon juice and enough boiling water to make 2⅔ cups. Cool for 20 minutes. Spoon a thin covering of cool Jello into the base of a 6-cup charlotte mold, refrigerate for about 20 minutes or until set.

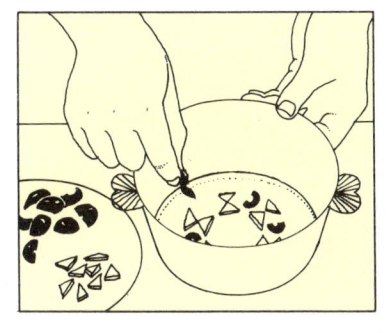

2 When set, arrange the cherry quarters and angelica triangles on top. Carefully spoon over cool liquid Jello to a depth of about 1 inch. Refrigerate for about 30 minutes to set, together with the remaining Jello.

3 Bring the milk slowly to the boil with the vanilla bean; take off the heat, cover and leave to infuse for at least 10 minutes. Put the water in a small bowl and sprinkle in the gelatine. Stand the bowl over a saucepan of hot water and heat gently until dissolved. Remove the bowl from the water and set aside to cool slightly.

4 Using a wooden spoon, beat together the egg yolks and sugar until well mixed, then stir in the strained milk. Return to the pan and cook gently, stirring all the time until the custard is thick enough to just coat the back of the spoon—do *not* boil. Pour into a large bowl, stir in the gelatine and allow to cool for 30 minutes.

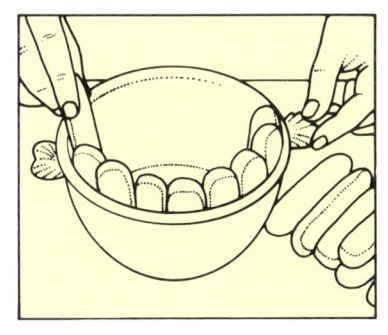

5 Trim the ladyfingers so that they just fit the mold; reserve the trimmings. Stand the fingers closely together, sugar side out, around the edge of the mold.

6 Lightly whip the cream and stir into the cool custard. Place the bowl in a roasting pan. Pour in enough iced water to come halfway up its sides. Stir occasionally for about 10 minutes until the custard is on the point of setting and has a *thick* pouring consistency. Pour gently into the lined mold without disturbing the ladyfingers.

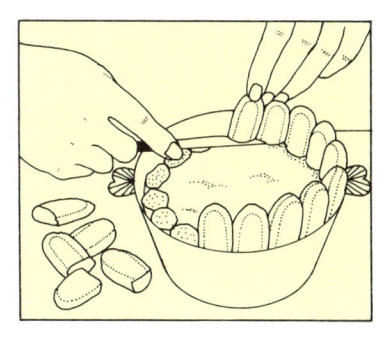

7 Trim the ladyfingers level with the custard. Lay the trimmings together with the reserved trimmings on top of the custard. Cover with plastic wrap and refrigerate for at least 3 hours to set.

8 To turn out, using fingertips, ease the ladyfingers away from the mold, then tilt it slightly to allow an airlock to form between the two. Dip the base of the mold in hot water for about 5 seconds only—to loosen the Jello. Invert the pudding on to a damp plate, shake mold gently, then ease it carefully off the finished charlotte.

9 Loosen the remaining set Jello by dipping the bowl in hot water for a few seconds only. Turn out on to a board lined with damp parchment. Moisten a large knife and chop the Jello into small pieces. Spoon the Jello around the charlotte russe.

CHARLOTTE RUSSE

A classic French dessert, this charlotte Russe (Russian for charlotte) is made with a filling of *crème bavarois*—a rich vanilla-flavored egg custard. Sometimes the custard is flavored with chocolate, almond-flavored liqueur or kirsch. Fresh raspberries can also be added when they are in season.

IRRESISTIBLE DESSERTS

TIPSY CAKE

| 0.30* | $ | ✽ | 690 cals |

* plus overnight refrigeration
1½ lbs stale sponge cake
¾ cup sherry
¾ cup strawberry or sieved raspberry jam
¾ cup walnuts, chopped
⅔ cup whipping cream
crystallized violets, to decorate

1. Crumble the cake into a bowl. Add the sherry, jam and walnuts and mix well.

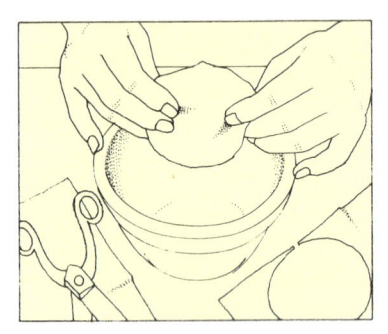

2. Line the base of a 4-cup pudding basin with a circle of baking parchment.

3. Spoon the mixture into the pudding basin, cover with wax paper and place heavy weights on top. Chill in the refrigerator overnight.

4. The next day, remove the weights, turn the cake out on to a serving plate and remove the parchment circle.

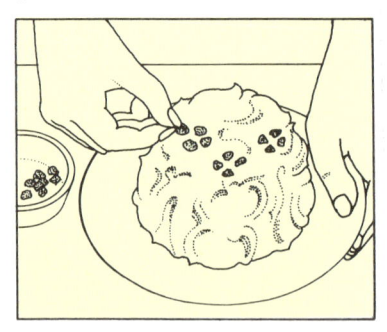

5. Whip the cream until standing in soft peaks, then swirl over the cake to cover it completely. Decorate with crystallized violets. Refrigerate until serving time.

TIPSY CAKE

A kind of old-fashioned trifle, tipsy cake is rich and very boozy. Originally made with Madeira wine and brandy rather than the sherry used here, it was also sometimes covered in a thick egg custard before being smothered with cream. The crystallized violets used to decorate this pretty dessert look very delicate. Years ago they would have used fresh flowers to decorate a tipsy cake for a special occasion—and you can do the same today if you wish. Pale green pistachio nuts or toasted blanched almonds can also be used for decoration; either would make a striking contrast with the flowers and cream.

If you are making tipsy cake for a special occasion—it makes an eye-catching table centerpiece for a buffet party—it can be made up to the end of step 3 several days beforehand and stored in the refrigerator.

DINNER PARTY DESSERTS

IRRESISTIBLE DESSERTS

DINNER PARTY DESSERTS

COFFEE-NUT ICE CREAM

| 0.40* | 🍴 | $ $ | ✻ | 669 cals |

* plus at least 6 hours freezing and 30 minutes softening

Serves 4

| 1 cup shelled hazelnuts |
| 2 Tbsp plus 4 tsp coffee-flavored liqueur |
| 1 Tbsp instant coffee powder |
| 2⅔ cups whipping cream |
| 1 cup confectioners sugar, sifted |

1 Toast the hazelnuts under the broiler for a few minutes, shaking the pan constantly so that the nuts brown evenly.

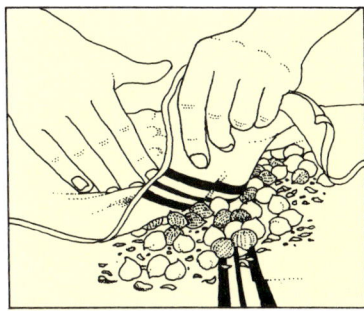

2 Tip the nuts into a clean tea-towel and rub to remove the skins. Chop finely.

3 Mix 2 Tbsp coffee liqueur and coffee powder together in a bowl. Stir in the chopped nuts, reserving a few for decoration.

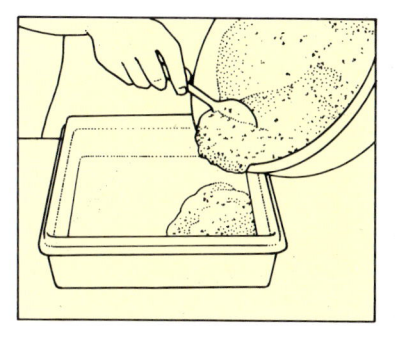

4 In a separate bowl, whip the cream and confectioners sugar together until thick. Fold in the nut mixture, then turn into a shallow freezerproof container. Freeze for 2 hours until ice crystals form around the edge of the ice cream.

5 Turn the ice cream into a bowl and beat thoroughly for a few minutes to break up the ice crystals. Return to the freezer container, cover and freeze for at least 4 hours, preferably overnight (to allow enough time for the flavors to develop).

6 To serve, transfer the ice cream to the refrigerator for 30 minutes to soften slightly, then scoop into individual glasses. Spoon 1 tsp coffee liqueur over each serving and sprinkle with the remaining nuts. Serve immediately.

ICE CREAM MAKERS

It is always satisfying to make your own ice cream, but sometimes the texture is disappointing because large ice crystals have formed in the mixture due to insufficient beating. Electric ice cream makers help enormously with this problem: they are not very expensive and are well worth buying if you like to make ice cream for occasions such as dinner parties when everything needs to be as near perfect as possible. The mixture is placed in the machine, which is then put into the freezer and switched on (the cable is flat so that the freezer door can close safely on it). Paddles churn the mixture continuously until the mixture is thick, creamy and velvety smooth—a consistency that is almost impossible to obtain when beating by hand.

IRRESISTIBLE DESSERTS

Banana Cheesecake

0.40* $ $ ✱*
428–570 cals

* plus 3–4 hours chilling; freeze after step 5. Defrost in refrigerator overnight, then continue with step 6.

Serves 6–8

18 gingersnaps
½ cup unsalted butter, melted and cooled
8 oz cream cheese
⅔ cup sour cream
3 bananas
2 Tbsp honey
1 Tbsp chopped preserved ginger (with syrup)
3 tsp gelatine
4 Tbsp lemon juice
banana slices and preserved ginger slices, to decorate

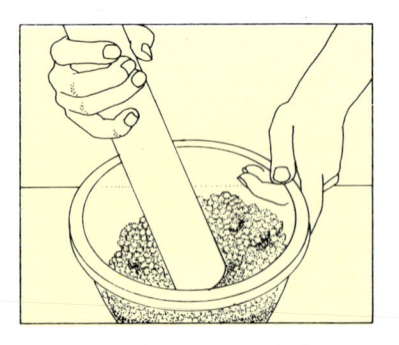

1 Make the crust. Crush the gingersnaps finely using a food processor or blender. Stir in the melted butter.

2 Press the mixture over the base of an 8-inch springform pan. Chill in the refrigerator for about 30 minutes.

3 Meanwhile, make the filling. Beat the cheese and cream together until well mixed. Peel and mash the bananas, then beat into the cheese mixture with the honey and ginger.

4 Sprinkle the gelatine over the lemon juice in a small heatproof bowl. Stand the bowl over a saucepan of hot water and heat gently until dissolved.

5 Stir the dissolved gelatine slowly into the cheesecake mixture, then spoon into the crumb-lined pan. Chill in the refrigerator for about 3–4 hours until the mixture is set.

6 To serve, remove the cheesecake carefully from the pan and place on a serving plate. Decorate around the edge with banana and ginger slices. Serve as soon as possible or the banana will discolor.

DINNER PARTY DESSERTS

PROFITEROLES

1.10* | $ | ✱* | 685 cals

* plus 20 minutes cooling; freeze after step 5. Defrost in refrigerator overnight, then continue from step 6.

Serves 4

| ¼ cup butter or margarine |
| ⅔ cup water |
| ½ cup all-purpose flour |
| 2 eggs, lightly beaten |
| ⅔ cup whipping cream |
| confectioners sugar |
| 6 oz semisweet chocolate, broken into pieces |
| 1 Tbsp butter |
| 3 Tbsp milk |
| 3 Tbsp light corn syrup |

1 Make the choux pastry. Put the butter and water in a saucepan. Heat gently until the butter has melted, then bring to the boil. Remove the pan from the heat.

2 Tip the flour all at once into the hot liquid. Beat thoroughly with a wooden spoon, then return the pan to the heat.

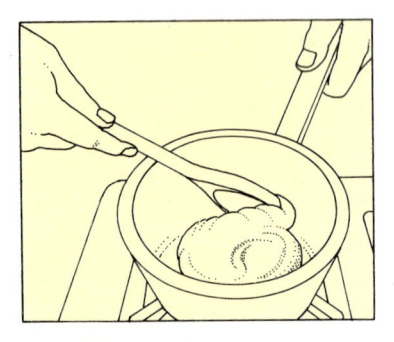

3 Continue beating the mixture until it is smooth and forms a ball in the center of the pan. (Take care not to over-beat or the mixture will become fatty.) Remove from the heat and leave the mixture to cool for a minute or two.

4 Beat in the egg, a little at a time, adding only just enough to give a piping consistency. It is important to beat the mixture vigorously at this stage to trap in as much air as possible. A hand-held electric mixer is ideal for this purpose. Continue beating until the mixture develops a sheen.

5 Dampen the surface of two or three baking sheets with water. Fill a pastry bag fitted with a medium plain nozzle with the choux pastry and pipe small balls, about the size of walnuts, on to the baking sheets.

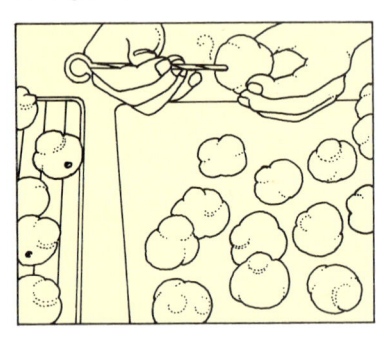

6 Bake in the oven at 400°F for 25–30 minutes until crisp. Make a hole in the bottom of each profiterole to release the steam, and leave to cool on a wire rack for 20 minutes.

7 Whip the cream until stiff. Fill a pastry bag fitted with a medium plain nozzle with the cream, and use to fill the profiteroles.

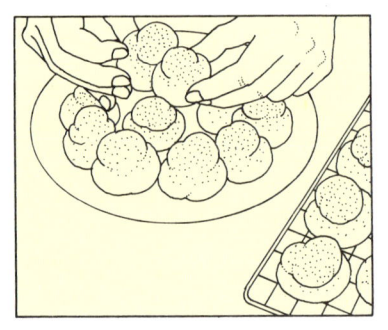

8 Dredge with confectioners sugar and pile the profiteroles into a pyramid shape.

9 To make the chocolate sauce, put the chocolate in a small bowl with the butter. Add the milk and syrup. Stand the bowl over a pan of warm water and heat gently, stirring, until the chocolate has melted and the sauce is warm.

10 Beat well, then pour a little chocolate sauce over the profiteroles and serve the rest separately. Serve immediately.

PROFITEROLES

A pyramid of luscious, cream-filled profiteroles coated in a rich chocolate sauce is an all-time favorite dinner party dessert. Take care when making choux pastry that the dough does not become too fatty through over-beating, as this will result in heavy-textured profiteroles. For the same reason, when adding the eggs in stage 4, watch the consistency of the dough carefully. Eggs vary in size even within their grade, and flour absorbs different amounts of liquid depending on its freshness and the temperature of the room you are working in. If the dough begins to feel slack, you do not need to add all of the beaten egg.

DINNER PARTY DESSERTS

ORANGES EN SURPRISE

0.50* $ $ ✳ 392 cals

* plus at least 4 hours (preferably overnight) freezing
6 large oranges
1⅓ cups whipping cream
¾ cup confectioners sugar
6 Tbsp orange-flavored liqueur
6 Tbsp chunky orange marmalade
fresh bay leaves or chocolate rose leaves, to decorate (optional)

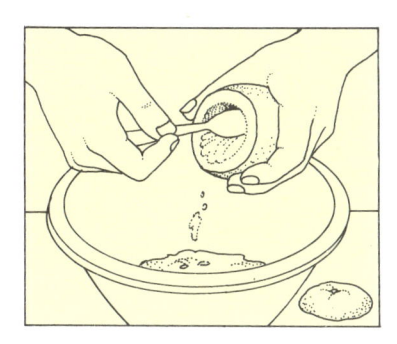

1 Cut a slice off the top of each orange and reserve. Scoop out all the flesh, seeds and juice from the oranges and discard (the juice can be used for drinking or in other recipes). Wash, then dry thoroughly. Set aside.

2 Whip the cream with the confectioners sugar until standing in stiff peaks. Mix together the liqueur and marmalade, then fold into the cream until evenly distributed.

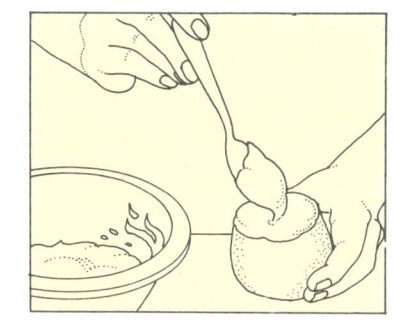

3 Spoon the cream mixture into the orange shells, mounding it up so that it protrudes over the top. Freeze for at least 4 hours, preferably overnight (to allow the flavors to develop). Serve straight from the freezer, decorated with reserved orange lids, bay or chocolate rose leaves.

IRRESISTIBLE DESSERTS

DINNER PARTY DESSERTS

HOT CHOCOLATE SOUFFLÉ

1.00 | $ $ | 629 cals

Serves 4

| $\frac{1}{3}$ cup sugar, plus extra to coat |
| 2 oz semisweet chocolate, broken into pieces |
| 3 Tbsp brandy |
| 2 Tbsp butter or margarine |
| 2 Tbsp all-purpose flour |
| $\frac{2}{3}$ cup milk |
| 3 egg yolks and 4 egg whites |
| confectioners sugar |
| hot chocolate sauce (see page 153), to serve |

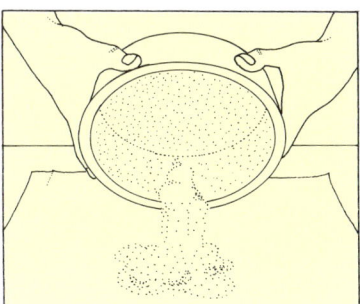

1 Coat the inside of a greased 6-inch soufflé dish with sugar. Shake off the excess sugar.

2 Put the chocolate and brandy in a heatproof bowl standing over a pan of simmering water. Heat gently until melted. Remove bowl from the pan.

3 Melt the butter in a separate saucepan, add the flour and cook for 2 minutes, stirring all the time. Remove from the heat and gradually add the milk, then return to the heat and bring to the boil, stirring. Simmer for 2 minutes until thick and smooth.

4 Remove the pan from the heat and stir in the sugar, melted chocolate and egg yolks, one at a time.

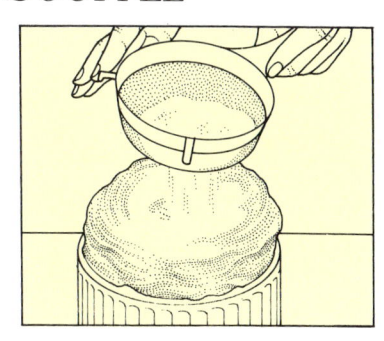

5 Whisk the egg whites until stiff, then fold into the chocolate mixture. Turn into the prepared soufflé dish and bake immediately in the oven at 400°F for 35 minutes until well risen. Dredge with confectioners sugar and serve the soufflé immediately, with hot chocolate sauce handed separately.

TIPS ON MAKING A HOT SOUFFLÉ

Making a hot soufflé is easier than you think. Here are a few helpful hints for success every time:
● Preheat the oven to the required temperature before starting the recipe, and preheat a baking sheet on the center shelf at the same time. This ensures that the soufflé starts cooking immediately it is put into the oven. Remove any shelves above the center shelf before baking to allow room for rising.
● Make sure the egg whites are whisked stiffly before folding them into the sauce mixture. To test if they are stiff enough, turn the bowl upside down— they should not drop.
● To lighten the sauce mixture, fold a tablespoon of the stiffly whisked egg whites into the sauce before folding in the rest.

47

IRRESISTIBLE DESSERTS

Marbled Apricot Soufflé

|2.00*| $ $ * |439–585 cals|

* plus overnight soaking, 1½ hours cooling and 4 hours setting

Serves 6–8

2 cups dried apricots, soaked overnight in cold water
¾ cup water
1 cup sugar
2 Tbsp almond-flavored liqueur
3 tsp gelatine
4 eggs, separated
1⅓ cups whipping cream
few drops of orange food coloring
almond or vanilla wafers and whipped cream, to decorate

1 Prepare a 6-inch soufflé dish: cut a double thickness of baking parchment long enough to go around the outside of the dish and 2–3 inches deeper. Secure the dish around the outside with paper clips and string.

2 Drain the soaked dried apricots, then put them in a saucepan with 8 Tbsp of the water and ⅓ cup of the sugar. Heat gently until the sugar has dissolved, then cover and simmer for about 30 minutes until tender. Leave to cool slightly, then rub through a sieve or purée in a blender. Stir in the liqueur and leave to cool for about 30 minutes.

3 Meanwhile, place the remaining water in a small heatproof bowl and sprinkle in the gelatine. Stand the bowl over a saucepan of hot water and heat gently until dissolved. Remove the bowl from the water and cool slightly.

4 Put the egg yolks and remaining sugar in a large heatproof bowl and stand over the pan of gently simmering water. Whisk until the mixture is thick and holds a ribbon trail, then remove from the heat and leave for about 1 hour until cold, whisking occasionally.

5 Whip the cream until it will stand in soft peaks. Whisk the egg whites until stiff.

6 Stir the gelatine liquid into the apricot purée, then fold this into the egg yolk mixture until evenly blended. Next fold in the whipped cream, then egg whites.

7 Transfer half the mixture to a separate bowl and tint with the food coloring.

8 Put alternate spoonfuls of the two mixtures into the prepared soufflé dish. Level the surface, then chill in the refrigerator for at least 4 hours until set.

9 Carefully remove the paper from the edge of the soufflé. Press the crushed wafers around the exposed edge. Decorate top with wafers and whipped cream.

DINNER PARTY DESSERTS

IRRESISTIBLE DESSERTS

Meringue Surprise Framboise

0.45* 🍴🍴 $ $ ✳

370–493 cals

* plus 1 hour cooling and at least 4 hours freezing

Serves 6–8

1 Tbsp arrowroot
6 egg yolks and 2 egg whites
⅓ cup sugar
1 tsp vanilla extract
1½ cups milk
1⅓ cups whipping cream
16 baby meringues
¾ lb frozen raspberries
juice of 1 lemon
confectioners sugar to taste
3 Tbsp Framboise

1 Put the arrowroot in a heat-proof bowl and blend to a paste with the egg yolks, sugar and vanilla extract.

2 Scald the milk by bringing it up to boiling point, then stir slowly into the egg yolk mixture.

3 Stand the bowl over a pan of gently simmering water and stir until the custard is thick enough to coat the back of a wooden spoon.

4 Remove from the heat, cover the surface of the custard closely with plastic wrap to prevent a skin forming and leave for 1 hour.

5 Whip the cream until it just holds its shape, then fold into the cold custard. Whisk the egg whites until stiff, then fold in until evenly incorporated.

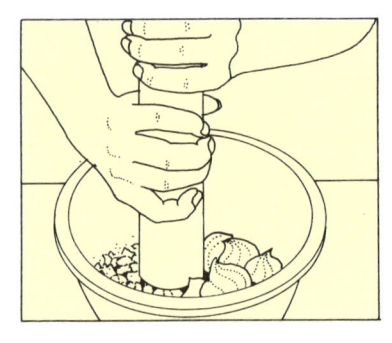

6 Crush 10 of the meringues roughly and fold into the custard mixture until evenly distributed.

7 Line the base of a 6-inch Charlotte mold or soufflé dish with parchment paper. Pour in the custard mixture, cover the mold, then freeze for at least 4 hours or overnight until solid.

8 Meanwhile, make the raspberry sauce. Reserve a few whole frozen raspberries for decoration.

9 Put the remaining frozen raspberries and the lemon juice in a heavy-bottomed saucepan and heat gently until defrosted, shaking the pan constantly.

10 Cook gently for 10 minutes, then tip into a sieve and press with the back of a spoon to extract as much juice as possible.

11 Sift the confectioners sugar into the raspberry juice, then stir in the liqueur. Leave until cold, taste.

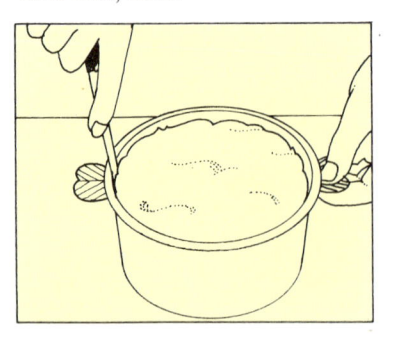

12 To serve, run a knife around the dessert in the mold, then carefully turn out on to a serving plate. Remove paper.

13 Pour a little of the sauce over the dessert, then decorate with the reserved raspberries and the remaining meringues. Serve at once, with the remaining sauce handed separately.

DINNER PARTY DESSERTS

IRRESISTIBLE DESSERTS

DINNER PARTY DESSERTS

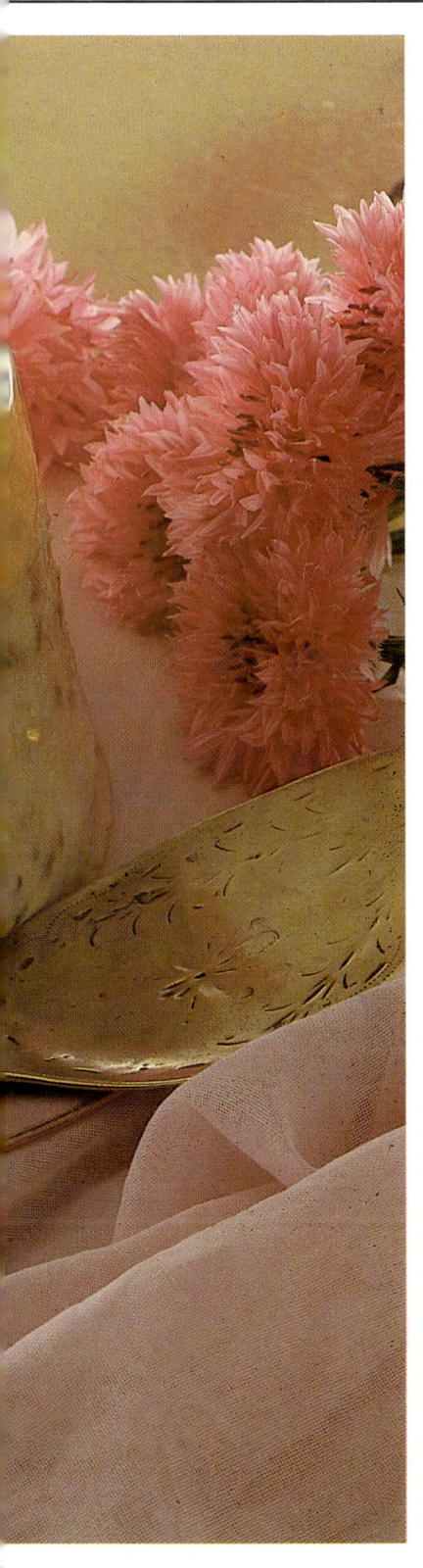

BANANA CHARTREUSE

| 4.00* | 🍳 | $ $ | 290–435 cals |

*plus 1½ hours cooling
Serves 4–6

3-oz package lemon Jello
1½ cups boiling water
3 bananas
juice of ½ a lemon
about 6 shelled pistachio nuts
3 tsp gelatine
4 Tbsp dark rum
⅔ cup whipping cream
⅔ cup confectioners sugar, sifted

1 Make the Jello according to the package instructions, using 1½ cups boiling water. Cool for 30 minutes.

2 Pour about one third of the Jello into a chilled 6-inch charlotte mold. Chill for 30 minutes until set.

3 Peel 1 banana, slice thinly, then sprinkle with a little lemon juice to prevent browning.

4 Arrange the banana slices on top of the set Jello in an attractive pattern. Cut the pistachios in half lengthways and place between or around the banana slices.

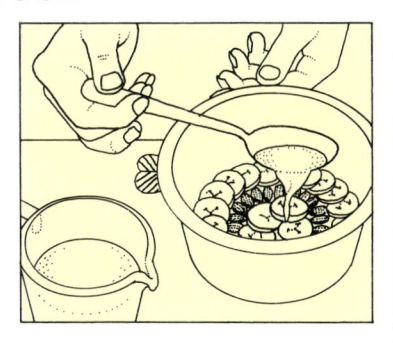

5 Slowly spoon over the remaining cool Jello, taking care not to dislodge the pattern of bananas and pistachios. Chill for 30 minutes until set.

6 Sprinkle the gelatine over the rum and remaining lemon juice in a small heatproof bowl. Stand the bowl over a saucepan of hot water and heat gently until dissolved. Cool for 5 minutes.

7 Whip the cream with the confectioners sugar. Peel and mash the remaining bananas, then combine with the cream and cooled gelatine liquid. Spoon on top of the set Jello and chill in the refrigerator for about 2 hours until set.

8 To serve, dip base of mold in hot water for a few seconds, then invert banana chartreuse on to a serving plate. Serve chilled.

CHARTREUSE
The word *chartreuse* in French culinary terms can mean several different things. It is the name of a yellow or green liqueur made by the monks at the abbey of Chartreuse. *En chartreuse* is a term used to describe a game bird which is stewed with cabbage. Or, as here, it can be used to describe a dessert made with Jello.

53

IRRESISTIBLE DESSERTS

Raspberry Walnut Torte

| 1.45* | 🍳 | $ $ | 539 cals |

* plus 30 minutes chilling
Serves 8

| 1 cup walnuts |
| $\frac{1}{2}$ cup unsalted butter |
| $\frac{1}{2}$ cup sugar |
| $1\frac{1}{4}$ cups all-purpose flour |
| 1 lb fresh raspberries |
| $\frac{2}{3}$ cup confectioners sugar |
| 2 Tbsp raspberry-flavored liqueur or kirsch (optional) |
| 2 cups whipping cream |

1 Grind the walnuts finely in a mouli grater, electric blender or food processor.

2 Cream the butter and sugar together until light and fluffy, then beat in the walnuts and flour. Divide the dough into three.

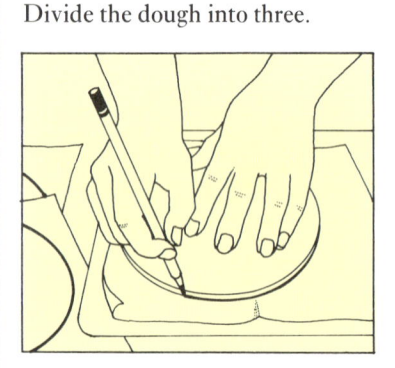

3 Draw three 8-inch circles on baking parchment. Place these on baking sheets.

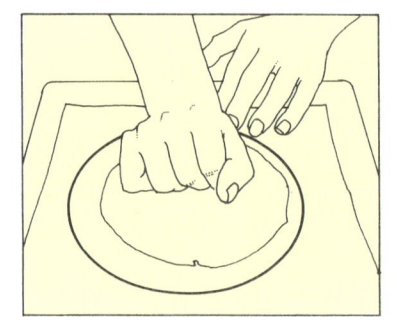

4 Put a piece of dough in the center of each circle and press with the heel of your hand until dough is same size as circle.

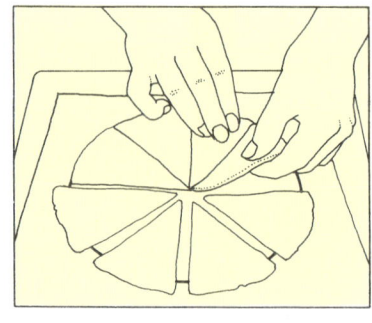

5 Cut one of the circles into eight triangles with a sharp knife and ease them slightly apart. Refrigerate the pastries for 30 minutes. Bake in the oven at

54

DINNER PARTY DESSERTS

375°F for 15–20 minutes. Leave to cool and harden for 10 minutes on the paper, then transfer to wire racks to cool completely.

6 Meanwhile, reserve one third of the whole raspberries for decoration. Put the rest in a bowl with the confectioners sugar and liqueur, if using. Crush the fruit with a fork, then leave to macerate while the pastry is cooling.

7 Assemble the torte just before serving. Whip the cream until thick, then fold in the crushed raspberries and juice. Stand one round of pastry on a flat serving plate and spread with half of the cream mixture. Top with the remaining round of pastry and the remaining cream mixture.

8 Arrange the triangles of pastry on top of the cream, wedging them in at an angle. Scatter the reserved whole raspberries in between. Serve as soon as possible.

55

Meringue Basket

6.00* $ $ 317–423 cals

*plus 20 minutes cooling

Serves 6–8

4 egg whites
2 cups confectioners sugar
1 small pineapple
3 bananas
1⅓ cups whipping cream
2 Tbsp kirsch
coarsely grated semisweet chocolate, to decorate

1 Line three baking sheets with baking parchment (turn rimmed baking sheets upside down and use the bases), and draw a 7½-inch circle on each. Turn the paper over so that the penciled circle is visible but does not come into contact with the meringues and mark them.

2 Place 3 egg whites in a clean, dry heatproof bowl, and place the bowl over a pan of simmering water. Sift in 1½ cups of the confectioners sugar.

3 Whisk the egg whites and sugar vigorously over the simmering water until the mixture stands in very stiff peaks. Do not allow the bowl to get too hot or the meringue will crust around edges.

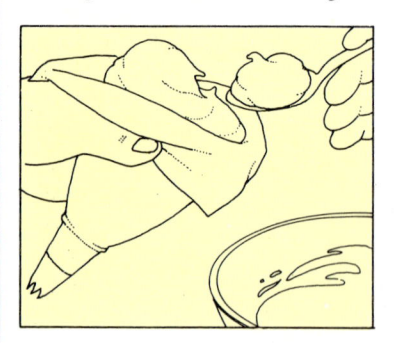

4 Fit a pastry bag with a large star nozzle. Spoon in one third of the meringue mixture. Secure the paper to the baking sheets with a little meringue.

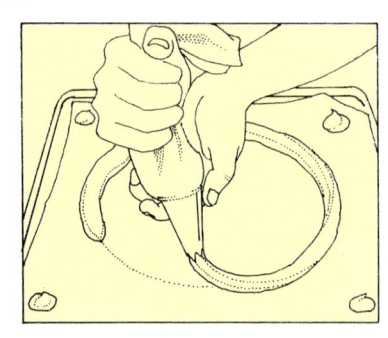

5 Pipe rings of meringue about ½-inch thick inside two of the circles on the paper.

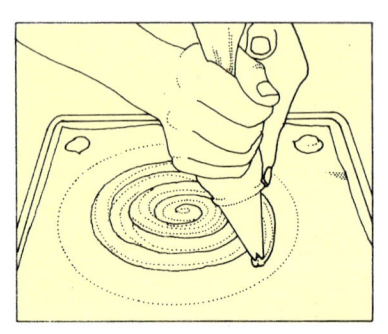

6 Fill the bag with the remaining meringue and, starting from center, pipe a continuous coil of meringue on the third sheet of paper. Place all in the oven at 200°F for 2½–3 hours to dry out.

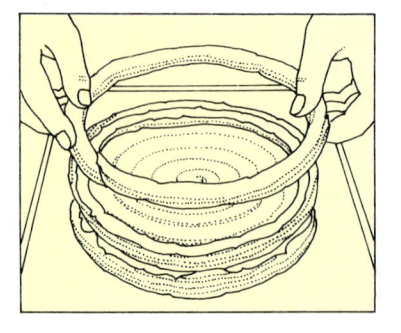

7 Use the remaining egg white and sugar to make meringue as before and put into the pastry bag. Remove the cooked meringue rings from the paper and layer up on the base, piping a ring of fresh meringue between each. Return to oven for a further 1½–2 hours. Slide on to a wire rack and peel off paper when cool.

8 Cut the pineapple across into ½-inch slices and snip off skin. Cut out core and divide flesh into bite-size chunks. Peel bananas and cut into ½-inch slices. Mix the fruits together, reserving a little pineapple and banana for decoration.

9 Just before serving, stand the meringue shell on a flat serving plate. Lightly whip the cream and fold in the kirsch; spoon half into the base of the basket and top with the fruit. Whirl the remaining cream over the top and decorate with the reserved pineapple, banana and the grated chocolate.

MAKING MERINGUES

There are three basic types of meringue. *Meringue suisse* is the most common and the most simple—egg whites are stiffly whisked, then sugar is folded in. *Meringue cuite* is the type of meringue used for this basket. It is firmer than *meringue suisse* and therefore better able to hold up when filled with fruit and cream as here. Although its name suggests that it is cooked, it is in fact only whisked over hot water before being baked in the same way as *meringue suisse*. *Meringue italienne* is made by combining sugar syrup with egg whites; it is difficult to make, and mostly used by professionals.

DINNER PARTY DESSERTS

IRRESISTIBLE DESSERTS

Traditional and Everyday Desserts

Here you will find the family favorites which everyone enjoys whenever you make them, but which tend to get forgotten when there are so many new things to try. Traditional pies and tarts are here, plus the more old-fashioned trifles and cobblers. Serve them for everyday desserts, or at a dinner party. You'll be surprised how much your family and friends will welcome a delicious reminder of the past.

TRADITIONAL AND EVERYDAY DESSERTS

ENGLISH TRIFLE

1.00* $ $ 604 cals

* plus 30 minutes cooling and 12 hours chilling

| 2½ cups milk |
| ½ vanilla bean |
| 2 eggs |
| 2 egg yolks |
| 2 Tbsp sugar, plus extra for sprinkling |
| 8 ladyfingers |
| ½ cup apricot jam |
| 1 cup macaroons, lightly crushed |
| ⅓ cup sherry |
| 1⅓ cups whipping cream |
| ½ cup glacé cherries, halved |
| ⅓ cup sliced almonds, toasted |

1 Heat the milk with the vanilla bean until it reaches boiling point. Remove from the heat, cover and leave to infuse for about 20 minutes.

2 Beat together the eggs, egg yolks and 2 Tbsp sugar. Strain milk on to the mixture. Return to pan and cook over gentle heat for about 10 minutes without boiling, stirring all the time until the custard thickens slightly.

3 Pour the custard into a bowl, lightly sprinkle the surface with sugar, then leave to cool for 30 minutes.

4 Pull the ladyfingers in half and sandwich together with jam, cut up and place in a 2-quart shallow serving dish with the macaroons. Spoon over the sherry, then pour over the cold custard. Cover and refrigerate for about 12 hours.

5 Whip the cream until stiff. Top the custard with half the cream and pipe the remaining cream on top. Decorate the trifle with cherries and sliced almonds before serving.

MAKING EGG CUSTARD

Egg custard is traditional in an English trifle, but curdling can be a problem. Use a heavy-bottomed pan (cast iron is best) and keep the heat very gentle until the mixture thickens. Don't be impatient to hurry the thickening along by increasing the heat—this will almost certainly result in a lumpy or grainy custard. A useful tip is to combine the eggs and sugar with 1 tsp cornstarch before adding the milk. Cornstarch helps stabilize the mixture, but it does not taste in the finished trifle.

Lime Meringue Pie

| 1.35* | $ | 520 cals |

* plus 30 minutes chilling

shortcrust pastry (see page 152) for 8-inch fluted tart pan
2 limes
½ cup sugar
3 Tbsp cornstarch
2 eggs, separated
1 Tbsp butter
⅔ cup sugar
lime slices, to decorate (optional)
light cream, to serve

1 Roll out the pastry on a floured work surface and use to line an 8-inch fluted tart pan. Refrigerate for 30 minutes. Bake in the oven at 400°F for 10–15 minutes.

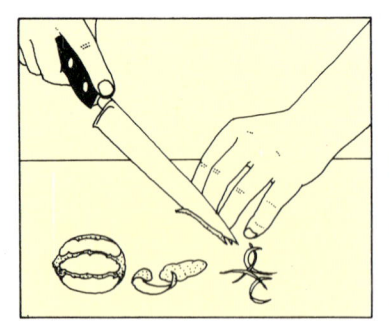

2 Pare a few strips of lime peel, shred finely, blanch in boiling water for 1 minute, drain, cool.

3 Finely grate the remaining rind from the limes into a small saucepan. Strain the juice; make 1⅓ cups liquid with water and add to the pan with the ½ cup sugar. Heat gently to dissolve the sugar.

4 Blend the cornstarch with 2 Tbsp water to a smooth paste. Add some of the heated liquid and stir. Return to the pan and boil for 2 minutes, stirring all the time. Cool slightly, then beat in the egg yolks and butter. Pour into the warm pastry.

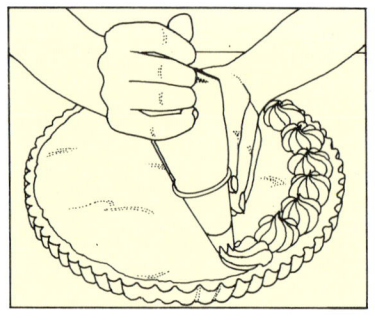

5 Whisk the egg whites until stiff, then fold in the remaining sugar. Spread a thin layer of meringue over the pie, then pipe the rest around the edge.

6 Bake in the oven at 300°F for about 45 minutes until the meringue is crisp and lightly browned.

7 Decorate with the shredded lime rind and slices (if using). Serve the pie warm, with cream.

Bakewell Pudding

| 0.45 | $ | 659–933 cals |

Serves 4–6

8 oz frozen puff pastry, thawed, or shortcrust pastry (see page 152) for a 9-inch pie pan
3 Tbsp raspberry jam
1½ cups ground almonds
⅔ cup sugar
¼ cup unsalted butter
3 eggs, beaten
¼ tsp almond extract
light cream or custard sauce

1. Roll out the pastry on a floured surface and use to line a 9-inch pie dish.

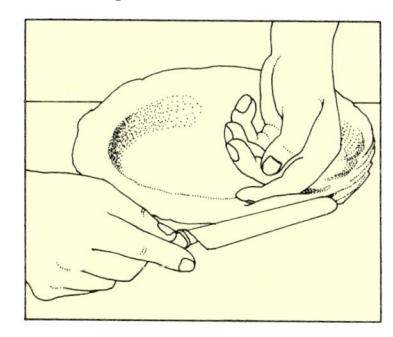

2. Crimp the edge of the pastry in the pie dish with the back of a knife.

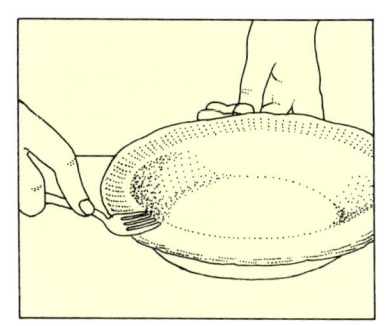

3. Mark the rim with the prongs of a fork. Brush the jam over the base. Chill in the refrigerator while making the filling.

4. Make the filling. Beat the almonds with the sugar, butter, eggs and almond extract.

5. Pour the filling over the jam and spread it evenly. Bake in the oven at 400°F for 30 minutes or until the filling is set. Serve warm or cold, with cream or custard sauce.

BAKEWELL PUDDING

This rich pudding was first created by the cook at an inn in Bakewell, Derbyshire in 1859. It is still made in the town today, according to a secret recipe. Our version is like the original, and not to be confused with the similar but drier Bakewell tart, which is made with bread or cake crumbs.

IRRESISTIBLE DESSERTS

OLD-FASHIONED MAPLE PIE

1.00 $ | 528–721 cals

Serves 4–6

1¼ cups all-purpose flour
pinch of salt
3 Tbsp sugar
¼ cup butter or margarine
2 Tbsp lard
1–2 Tbsp iced water
1 cup maple syrup
finely grated rind and juice of 1 lemon
1½ cups fresh white breadcrumbs
a little beaten egg or milk, to glaze
whipped cream, to serve

1 Place the flour and salt into a bowl, then stir in the sugar. Cut in half the butter or margarine with the lard until the mixture resembles fine cornmeal. Add enough iced water to mix to a firm dough.

2 Gather the dough together with your fingers and form into a ball, then roll out on a floured surface and use to line an 8-inch loose-bottomed fluted tart pan. Reserve the pastry trimmings. Chill in the refrigerator while making the filling.

3 Make the filling. Warm the maple syrup in a heavy-bottomed pan with the remaining butter and the lemon rind and juice.

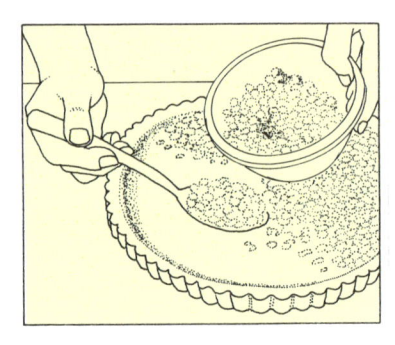

4 Sprinkle the breadcrumbs evenly over the pastry, then slowly pour in the melted syrup.

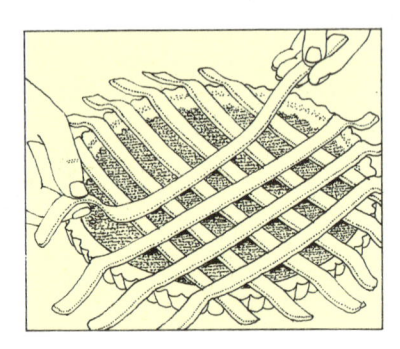

5 Make strips from the reserved pastry trimmings and place these over the tart in a lattice pattern, brushing the ends with water to stick them to the pastry. Glaze with a little beaten egg or milk.

6 Bake in the oven at 375°F for about 25 minutes until the filling is just set. Serve warm, with whipped cream.

TRADITIONAL AND EVERYDAY DESSERTS

Fruit Spongecakes

0.50 $ | 473 cals

Serves 4

1 cup shredded suet
2 cups fresh white breadcrumbs
1/3 cup light raisins
1/3 cup dark raisins
pinch of ground cinnamon
pinch of ground cloves
pinch of grated nutmeg
1/3 cup sugar
1/2 tsp baking powder
pinch of salt
2 eggs, beaten
custard sauce, to serve (see page 146)

1 Mix the suet with the breadcrumbs and add the fruit, spices, sugar, baking powder and salt. Mix very well together, then stir in the eggs.

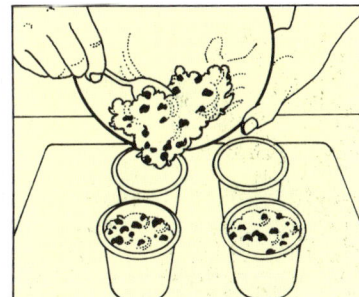

2 Pour into four greased individual soufflé dishes placed on a baking tray and bake in the oven at 350°F for about 30 minutes. Turn out and serve hot with custard sauce.

IRRESISTIBLE DESSERTS

TRADITIONAL AND EVERYDAY DESSERTS

SPICED APPLE AND PLUM CRUMBLE

| 1.10* | $ | ✳ | 402 cals |

* plus 30 minutes cooling
1 lb plums
1½ lb cooking apples
⅓ cup butter or margarine
⅔ cup sugar
1½ tsp allspice
1¼ cups whole wheat flour
½ cup blanched hazelnuts, toasted and chopped

1 Using a sharp knife, cut the plums in half and then carefully remove the stones.

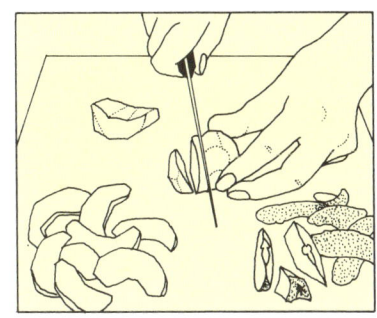

2 Peel, quarter, core and slice the apples. Place in a medium saucepan with 2 Tbsp butter, half the sugar, and about 1 tsp allspice.

3 Cover the pan and cook gently for 15 minutes until the apples begin to soften. Stir in the plums and turn into a 2-quart shallow ovenproof dish. Leave to cool for about 30 minutes.

4 Stir the flour and remaining allspice well together, then cut in the remaining butter until the mixture resembles fine cornmeal. Stir in the rest of the sugar with the chopped hazelnuts.

5 Spoon the crumble mixture over the fruit and bake in the oven at 350°F for about 40 minutes or until the top is golden, crisp and crumbly.

65

IRRESISTIBLE DESSERTS

Rich Chocolate Pie

1.00* | $ | 609 cals

* plus 30 minutes chilling and 4 hours setting

Serves 8

shortcrust pastry (see page 152) for a 9-inch pie
$\frac{2}{3}$ cup sugar
$\frac{1}{3}$ cup all-purpose flour
pinch of salt
2 cups milk
2 oz semisweet chocolate
3 egg yolks
3 Tbsp butter or margarine
1 tsp vanilla extract
1 cup whipping cream
chocolate curls (see page 143) or grated chocolate, to decorate

1. Roll out the pastry on a lightly floured surface and use to line a 9-inch loose-bottomed fluted tart pan. Crimp edges of pastry and refrigerate for 30 minutes.

2. Prick the pastry, then bake in the oven at 400°F for 10–15 minutes until lightly colored. Leave to cool.

3. While the pastry is cooling, mix the sugar with the flour and salt in a large saucepan and stir in the milk.

4. Break the chocolate into small pieces and add to the pan. Heat gently until the chocolate has melted, stirring continuously.

5. Whisk until the chocolate and milk are blended, then increase the heat and cook for about 10 minutes, stirring constantly. Remove saucepan from heat.

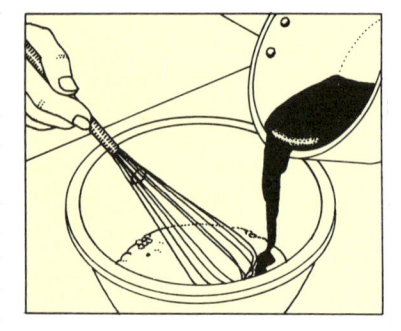

6. Beat the egg yolks and whisk in a small amount of the hot chocolate sauce.

7. Slowly pour the egg mixture into the saucepan, stirring rapidly. Cook over low heat stirring, for 10–15 minutes, until the mixture is very thick and creamy. Do not allow to boil.

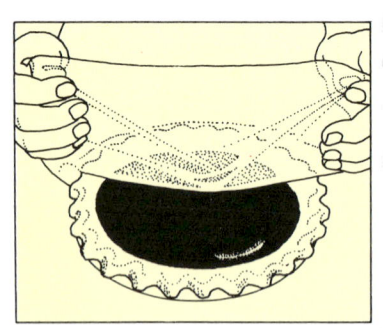

8. Remove from the heat. Stir in the butter and vanilla extract and pour into the pastry. Cover to prevent a skin forming and refrigerate for about 4 hours until set.

9. Just before serving, whip the cream lightly and spread it evenly over the chocolate filling. Decorate the top with chocolate curls or grated chocolate. Serve the pie chilled.

TRADITIONAL AND EVERYDAY DESSERTS

IRRESISTIBLE DESSERTS

TRADITIONAL AND EVERYDAY DESSERTS

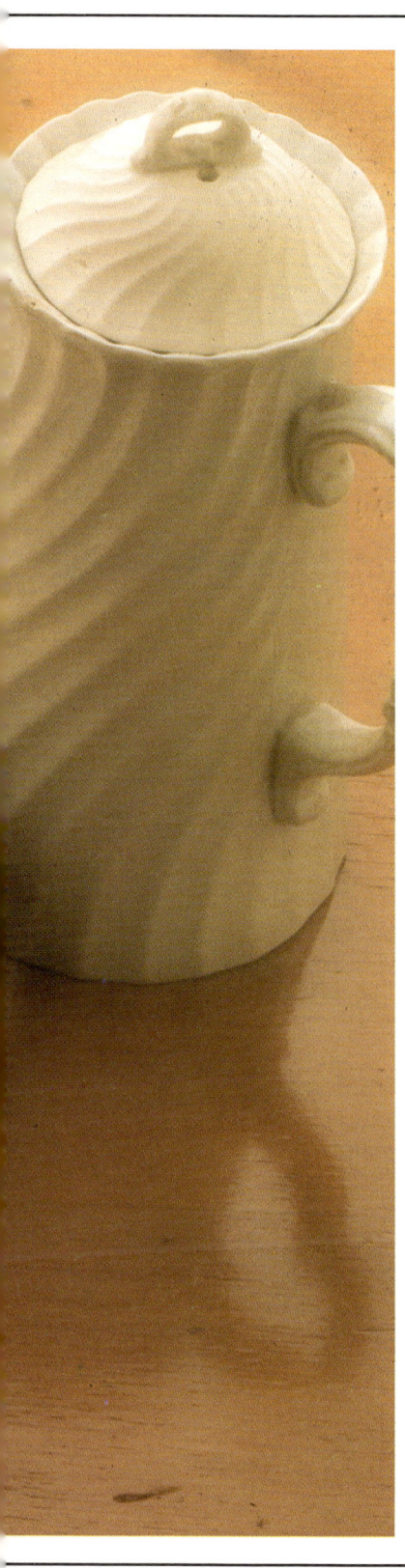

BLACKBERRY AND PEAR COBBLER

| 0.45 | $ | ✱ | 424 cals |

Serves 4

1 lb blackberries
1 lb ripe pears
¼ cup plus 2 Tbsp sugar
finely grated rind and juice of 1 lemon
½ tsp ground cinnamon
1½ cups self-rising flour
pinch of salt
¼ cup butter or margarine
⅔ cup milk plus extra to glaze

1 Pick over the blackberries and wash them. Peel and core the pears, then slice them thickly.

2 Put the blackberries and pears into a saucepan with the ¼ cup sugar, lemon rind and juice and the cinnamon. Poach gently for 15 or 20 minutes until the fruit is juicy and tender.

3 Meanwhile, place the flour and salt into the bowl. Cut in the butter, then stir in the remaining sugar. Gradually add the milk to mix to a fairly soft dough.

4 Roll out the dough on a floured work surface until ½ inch thick. Cut out rounds using a fluted 2-inch pastry cutter.

5 Put the fruit in a 10-inch deep dish pie pan and top with overlapping pastry rounds, leaving a gap in the center. Brush the top of the pastry rounds with milk. Bake in the oven at 425°F for 10–15 minutes until pastry is golden brown. Serve hot.

IRRESISTIBLE DESSERTS

Apple Almond Checkerboard

1.30 | $ | 784 cals

Serves 4

- 1½ lb cooking apples
- 1 tsp ground cinnamon
- 1¼ cups light brown sugar
- ½ cup butter, softened
- 2 eggs, beaten
- ¾ cup self-rising flour
- ¼ cup ground almonds
- ½ tsp almond extract
- 2 Tbsp milk
- ¼ cup sliced almonds
- confectioners sugar
- light cream, to serve

1 Peel, quarter and core the cooking apples, then slice them thickly into a 6-cup ovenproof dish. Combine the cinnamon with ¼ cup of the light brown sugar and scatter over the apples. Cover tightly with plastic wrap while preparing the topping.

2 Beat the butter and remaining sugar, creaming them together until fluffy. Gradually beat in eggs.

3 Fold in the flour, ground almonds, extract, and milk. Spread the mixture over the cooking apples.

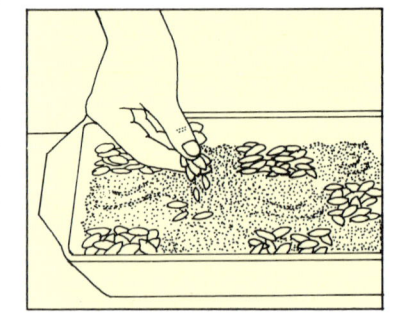

4 Place the sliced almonds on top in six squares to form a checkerboard effect. Bake in the oven at 350°F for 50–60 minutes until the apples are tender and the sponge risen and golden brown.

5 Sift confectioners sugar between the sliced almond squares. Serve with cream.

— VARIATION —

If liked, you can add ⅓ cup raisins to the apple mixture in the base of this delicious pudding. Grated orange or lemon zest added to the sponge topping also adds extra flavor—and goes particularly well with the cinnamon-flavored apples.

TRADITIONAL AND EVERYDAY DESSERTS

Noodle Pudding

| 1.00 | $ | 356 cals |

Serves 4

2 heaping cups, loosely packed dry fettuccine noodles
pinch of salt
1 egg
$\frac{1}{3}$ cup sugar
$\frac{1}{4}$ tsp ground cinnamon
finely grated rind of $\frac{1}{2}$ a lemon
$\frac{1}{3}$ cup currants
$\frac{1}{2}$ cup chopped almonds
2 Tbsp margarine

1 Drop the fettuccine into rapidly boiling salted water and cook for about 10 minutes until tender.

2 Drain into a sieve and rinse with plenty of hot water to remove excess starch. Drain well.

3 Whisk the egg and sugar together and stir in the cinnamon, rind, currants and nuts. Then stir in the fettuccine.

4 Melt the margarine in a 2-inch deep baking dish until hot but not smoking. Swirl around the dish to coat the sides and pour the excess into the noodle mixture.

5 Stir well and pour the mixture into the baking dish. Bake in the oven at 375°F for 45 minutes until set, crisp and brown on top. Serve hot.

IRRESISTIBLE DESSERTS

Crunchy Raspberry Cream

0.30* | $ | 481 cals

* plus 1 hour refrigeration and 30 minutes standing time

Serves 4

| 1⅓ cups rolled oats |
| 1⅓ cups whipping cream |
| 4 Tbsp honey |
| 3 Tbsp Scotch whisky |
| ¾ lb fresh raspberries, hulled |

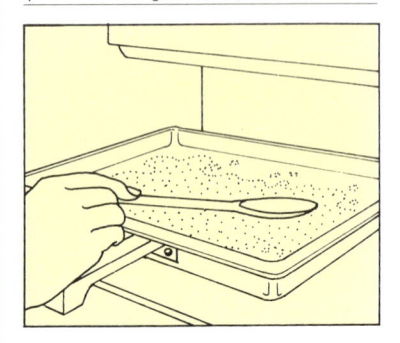

1 Place the oats in a pan and toast until golden brown, turning occasionally with a spoon. Leave for 15 minutes until cool.

2 Whip the cream until just standing in soft peaks, then stir in the honey, whisky and cooled toasted oats.

3 Reserve a few raspberries for decoration, then layer the remaining raspberries and fresh cream mixture in four tall glasses. Cover with plastic wrap and refrigerate for at least 1 hour.

4 Allow to come to room temperature for 30 minutes before serving. Decorate each glass with the reserved raspberries.

TRADITIONAL AND EVERYDAY DESSERTS

Cottage Cheese Tart

1.00 | $ | ✳ | 290–435 cals

Makes 8–12 slices

| 1½ cups all-purpose flour |
| pinch of salt |
| ½ cup plus 2 Tbsp butter or margarine |
| 1 egg yolk |
| 2 Tbsp cold water |
| 1 lb cottage cheese |
| 3 eggs, beaten |
| ½ cup currants |
| ¾ cup light brown sugar |
| finely grated rind of 1 lemon |

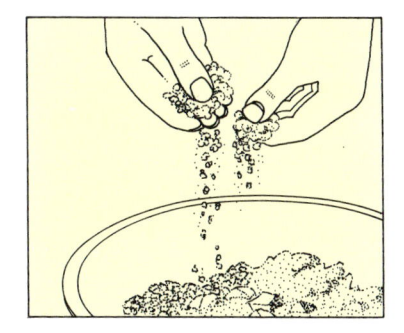

1 Make the pastry: place the flour and salt into a bowl, add ½ cup of the butter and cut in until the mixture resembles fine cornmeal. Stir in the egg yolk, and enough water to bind the mixture together. Form into a ball.

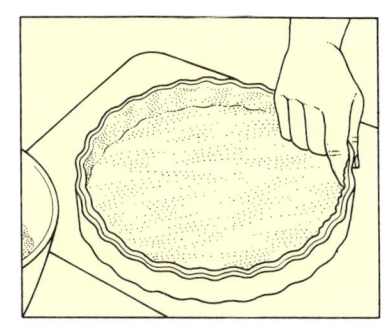

2 Roll out the pastry on a floured work surface. Use to line a 9-inch pie pan, then refrigerate while making the cottage cheese filling.

3 Put the cottage cheese in a bowl and stir in the eggs, followed by the currants, sugar and lemon rind. Melt the remaining butter and stir in until evenly mixed.

4 Pour the filling into the pastry and bake in the oven at 375°F for 45 minutes or until the filling is golden and set. Serve the tart warm or cold.

Danish "Peasant Girl in a Veil"

0.30* | $ | 601 cals

* plus cooling and 2–3 hours chilling

Serves 4

| ¼ cup butter or margarine |
| 3 cups fresh breadcrumbs |
| ½ cup brown sugar |
| 1½ lb cooking apples |
| 2 Tbsp water |
| juice of ½ a lemon |
| sugar to taste |
| ⅔ cup whipping cream |
| 2 oz grated chocolate, to decorate |

1 Melt the butter in a frying pan. Mix the crumbs and sugar together and fry in the hot butter until crisp, stirring frequently with a wooden spoon to prevent the crumbs from burning.

2 Peel, core and slice the apples. Put them in a saucepan with the water, lemon juice and some sugar to taste. Cover and cook gently for 10–15 minutes until they form a pulp. Leave to cool, then taste for sweetness.

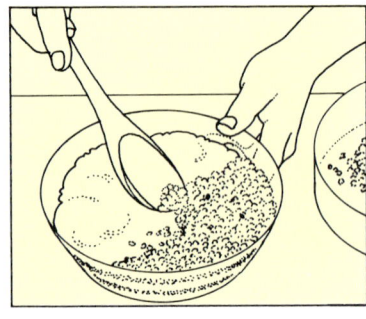

3 Put alternate layers of the fried crumb mixture and the apple pulp into a glass dish, finishing with a layer of crumbs. Refrigerate for 2–3 hours.

4 Whip the cream until stiff. Pipe over the top of the crumb mixture and decorate with grated chocolate. Serve chilled.

DANISH "PEASANT GIRL IN A VEIL"

This simple but delicious pudding of stewed apples layered with fried breadcrumbs and sugar is very similar to an apple crisp. In Denmark, where it is called *bondepige med slør*, it takes its name from the fact that the apple and crumbs are "veiled," or covered with cream. Like apple crisp, it is a country-style pudding, yet it tastes so good that it would be perfect for any type of special occasion, especially if made in a glass bowl so that the layers can be seen.

You can ring the changes by using different breadcrumbs. White breadcrumbs can of course be used, but whole grain gives a more nutty texture. In Denmark, rye bread would be used to make the crumbs.

TRADITIONAL AND EVERYDAY DESSERTS

IRRESISTIBLE DESSERTS

TRADITIONAL AND EVERYDAY DESSERTS

Magic Chocolate Pudding

| 0.45 | $ | 241–362 cals |

Serves 4–6

| ¼ cup butter or margarine |
| ½ cup sugar |
| 2 eggs, separated |
| ⅓ cup self-rising flour |
| 5 tsp cocoa |
| 1⅔ cups milk |

1. Cream the butter and sugar together until light and fluffy, then beat in the egg yolks.

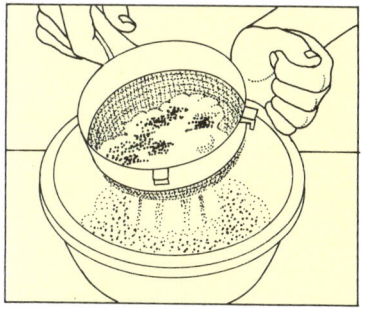

2. Sift the flour and cocoa together over the creamed mixture, then beat in until evenly mixed. Stir in the milk. Whisk the egg whites until stiff and fold into the mixture.

3. Pour into a greased 1-quart ovenproof dish. Bake in the oven at 350°F for 35–45 minutes until the top is set and spongy to the touch. This pudding will separate into a custard layer with a sponge topping. Serve hot.

MAGIC CHOCOLATE PUDDING

This delicious chocolate pudding, which is a great hit with children, is called "magic" because it separates magically during baking into a rich chocolate sauce at the bottom and a sponge cake on top.

77

IRRESISTIBLE DESSERTS

TRADITIONAL AND EVERYDAY DESSERTS

CHRISTMAS PLUM PUDDING

| 0.20* | $ $ | 611–736 cals |

* plus overnight maturing, 8 hours steaming, 2 hours cooling, 1 month maturing and 3 hours reheating

Serves 8–10

| $\frac{1}{3}$ cup dried figs |
| $\frac{1}{3}$ cup pitted prunes |
| $\frac{1}{3}$ cup pitted dates |
| $\frac{1}{3}$ cup glacé cherries |
| $\frac{2}{3}$ cup light raisins |
| $\frac{2}{3}$ cup currants |
| $\frac{2}{3}$ cup raisins |
| $\frac{1}{3}$ mixed candied fruit |
| 1 cup all-purpose flour |
| 1 cup dark brown sugar |
| 2 cups fresh whole wheat breadcrumbs |
| 2 cups shredded suet |
| 1 tsp allspice |
| 1 tsp salt |
| $\frac{1}{2}$ tsp grated nutmeg |
| 3 eggs |
| 5 Tbsp milk |
| 1 cup dark ale |
| 2 tsp lemon juice |
| custard sauce, to serve |

1 Roughly chop the figs, prunes, dates and cherries. Then, in a large bowl, mix all the dry ingredients together.

2 Whisk together the eggs, milk, ale and lemon juice. Stir into the dry ingredients, mixing well. Cover and refrigerate overnight.

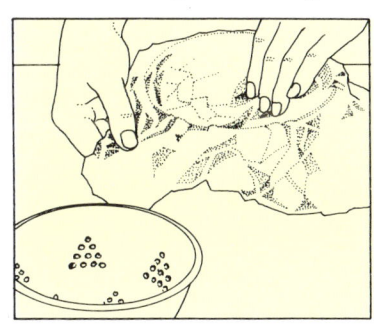

3 Line the two halves of a rice-steaming ball with foil so that it protrudes beyond the rim of each half, or generously grease a $2\frac{1}{2}$-quart steamed pudding mold. Fill with the mixture.

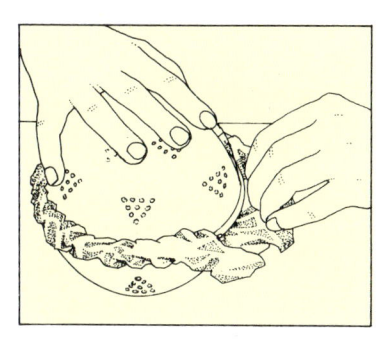

4 Close up the lined rice-steaming ball and twist the protruding foil edges together or place lid or foil on pudding mold.

5 Cook in a pan of rapidly boiling water reaching halfway up sides of mold for at least 8 hours, adding more water as necessary.

6 When cooked, remove pudding from water and leave to cool for at least 2 hours. Remove from the steaming ball or mold, unwrap foil, then rewrap in cheesecloth and fresh foil.

7 Store in a cool place to mature for at least 1 month. To serve, steam the pudding again for at least 3 hours. Serve with custard sauce.

79

IRRESISTIBLE DESSERTS

Lemon Surprise

| 4.30 | 🍳 | $ | 649 cals |

- 2½ cups self-rising flour
- ½ tsp salt
- 1½ cups shredded suet
- ¾ cup water
- ½ cup butter, cut into pieces
- ¾ cup light brown sugar
- 1 large lemon

1 Place the flour and salt into a bowl, then stir in the suet and enough cold water to make a light, elastic dough. Knead lightly until it is smooth.

2 Roll out two thirds of the pastry on a floured work surface to a circle, 1 inch larger all round than the top of a 1½-quart pudding mold.

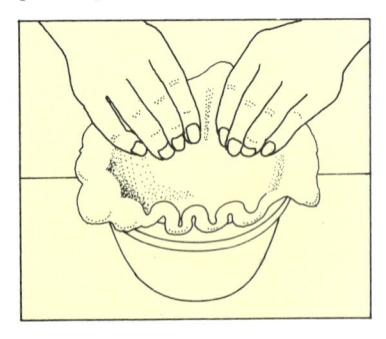

3 Use the rolled-out pastry to line the pudding mold. Put half the butter into the center with half the sugar.

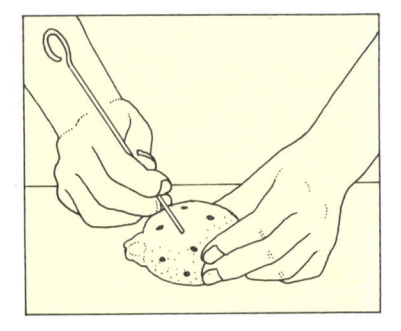

4 Prick the lemon all over with a skewer. Put the whole lemon on top of the butter and sugar. Add the remaining butter and sugar.

5 Roll out the remaining pastry to a circle to fit the top of the pudding. Dampen the edges and seal the lid. Cover with foil.

6 Place over a pan of boiling water and steam for about 4 hours, topping up the water as necessary. Remove foil and turn out on to a warm serving dish. During cooking the lemon inside the pudding bursts and produces a delicious lemon sauce. Each serving should have a piece of the lemon, which will be much softened by the cooking.

TRADITIONAL AND EVERYDAY DESSERTS

Jelly Roll with Hot Jam Sauce

2.30 $ 499 cals

Serves 4

1¼ cups self-rising flour
¼ tsp salt
¾ cup shredded suet
finely grated rind of 1 orange
3–4 Tbsp hot water
6 Tbsp raspberry jam plus 3 Tbsp
a little milk
finely grated rind of 1 orange
2 tsp arrowroot
⅔ cup fresh orange juice

1 Place the flour and salt into a bowl, then stir in the suet and orange rind. Gradually stir in the hot water until the dough binds together. Form into a ball, turn out on to a floured surface and knead lightly until smooth.

2 Roll out the dough on a floured work surface to a 10 × 8-inch oblong. Spread the first quantity of jam over the dough to ¼ inch of the edges. Brush the edges with milk.

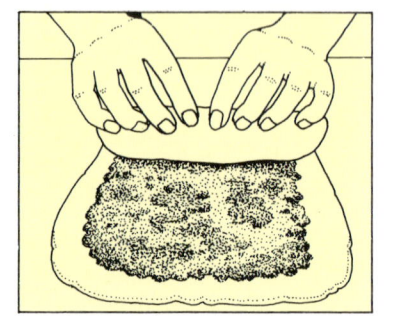

3 Roll up the pastry evenly like a jelly roll, starting from one short side.

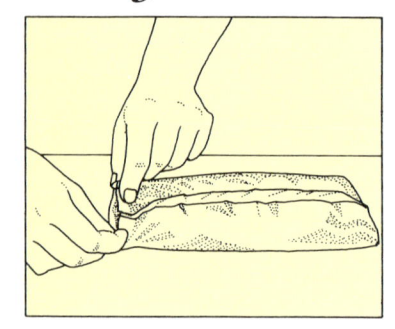

4 Place the roll, seam side down, on a sheet of greased foil measuring at least 12 × 9 inches. Wrap the foil loosely around the roll to allow room for expansion during cooking. Seal well.

5 Place the jelly roll in the top of a steamer over a pan of boiling water and steam for 1½–2 hours, topping up the water as necessary.

6 Just before serving, make the sauce. Put the remaining jam and orange rind in a heavy-based saucepan. Mix the arrowroot to a paste with a little of the orange juice, then stir the remaining orange juice into the pan. Heat gently until the jam has melted, then stir in the arrowroot paste and bring to the boil. Simmer until thickened, stirring constantly.

7 Unwrap the jelly roll and place on a warmed serving plate. Pour over the hot jam sauce and serve immediately.

Currant Roll

| 2.30 | 🍴 | $ | 604 cals |

Serves 4

2 cups fresh white breadcrumbs
½ cup plus 2 Tbsp self-rising flour
pinch of salt
¾ cup shredded suet
⅓ cup sugar
1 cup currants
finely grated rind of ½ a lemon
5–6 Tbsp milk
custard sauce, to serve

1. Place the breadcrumbs, flour, salt, suet, sugar, currants and lemon rind in a bowl. Stir well until thoroughly mixed.

2. Add enough milk to the dry ingredients to bind together, cutting it through with a palette knife until well mixed. Using one hand only, bring the ingredients together to form a soft, slightly sticky dough.

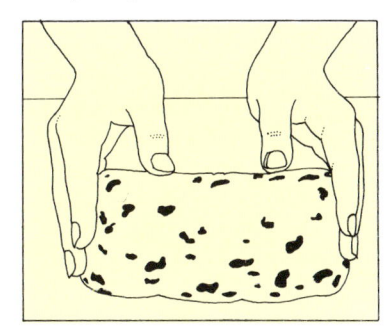

3. Turn the dough out on to a floured work surface. Dust lightly with flour, then knead gently until just smooth. Shape the dough into a neat roll about 6 inches in length.

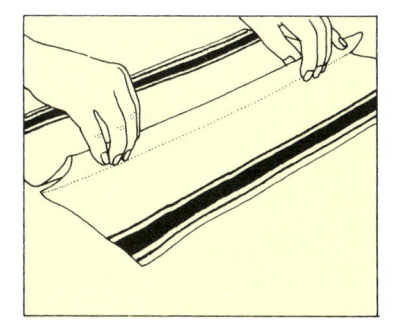

4. Make a 2-inch pleat across a fine-textured, color-fast teatowel or pudding cloth. Alternatively pleat together sheets of greased foil. Encase the roll in the cloth or foil, pleating the open edges tightly together. Tie the ends securely with string to form a cracker shape. Make a string handle across the top.

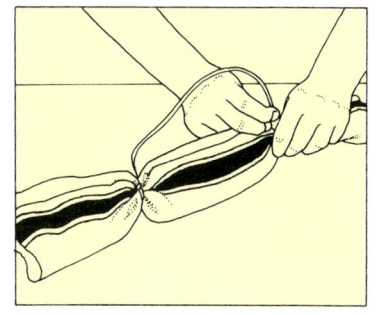

5. Lower the suet roll into a large saucepan, two-thirds full of boiling water, curling it if necessary to fit the pan. Cover the pan, lower the heat to a gentle boil and cook for 2 hours. Top up with boiling water at intervals.

6. Lift the currant roll out of the water. Snip the string and gently roll the pudding on to a serving plate. Decorate with lemon slices if liked and serve immediately, with custard sauce.

IRRESISTIBLE DESSERTS

Custards, Soufflés and Creams

Milk and eggs are not only two of the most nutritious of ingredients around, they're also immensely versatile. Don't dismiss them as being too basic for anything more than just a plain, everyday pudding. Take a look at the recipes in this chapter, and you'll see that with the addition of a few other ingredients and a little imagination, milk and eggs can make some of the most delicious desserts you've ever tasted.

CUSTARDS, SOUFFLÉS AND CREAMS

Crème Caramel

1.25* 414 cals

* plus 2 hours cooling, at least 2 hours chilling and 30 minutes standing time

Serves 4

$\frac{2}{3}$ cup plus 1 Tbsp sugar
$\frac{2}{3}$ cup water
$2\frac{1}{2}$ cups milk
4 eggs
$\frac{1}{4}$ tsp vanilla extract
light cream, to serve

1. Place the $\frac{2}{3}$ cup sugar in a small saucepan and carefully pour in the water. Heat the syrup gently, without boiling, until sugar has dissolved. Stir occasionally.

2. Place a 6-inch soufflé dish in a low oven to warm. Bring the syrup in the pan up to a fast boil and cook rapidly until the syrup starts to brown, shaking the pan to ensure it browns evenly. When caramel is golden, take off heat. Leave for a few seconds.

3. Immediately place the warmed dish on a heatproof surface. Carefully, pour in caramel and leave to cool for 30 minutes.

4. Scald the milk by heating to boiling point. Set aside. Place the eggs in a bowl and add the remaining sugar. Whisk until evenly mixed, then pour on the warm milk. Whisk in the vanilla extract, then strain the custard on to caramel.

5. Stand the dish in a roasting pan, then pour in enough hot water to come halfway up the sides of the dish. Bake in the oven at 325°F for about $1\frac{1}{2}$ hours. The custard should be just set and firm to the touch. Insert a skewer in the center; if clean when withdrawn, the custard is cooked.

6. Take the dish out of the pan and leave to cool for 2 hours. When cold, cover tightly with plastic wrap and refrigerate for 2–3 hours, preferably overnight.

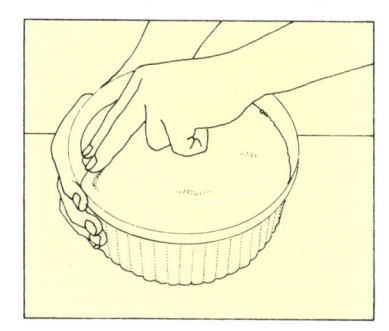

7. To serve, stand at room temperature for 30 minutes. Using the fingertips, gently loosen and ease the edges of the custard away from the dish. Place a rimmed serving dish over the crème caramel and, holding the two dishes firmly, invert.

8. Still holding the dishes together, give a few sharp sideways shakes until the suction is heard to release. Leave the soufflé dish upturned for a few minutes until all the caramel has trickled out. Then ease off and stand in a pan of hot water to soften remaining caramel: pour over the crème caramel, and serve accompanied with cream.

IRRESISTIBLE DESSERTS

Crème Brûlée

|1.25*| $ $ |423 cals|

* plus 1 hour cooling and 4–6 hours chilling

| $2\frac{2}{3}$ cups whipping cream |
| 4 egg yolks |
| $\frac{2}{3}$ cup sugar |
| 1 tsp vanilla extract |

1 Put the cream in the top of a double boiler or in a heatproof bowl over a pan of hot water. Heat gently; do not boil.

2 Meanwhile, put the egg yolks, $\frac{2}{3}$ cup of the sugar, and the vanilla extract in a bowl and beat thoroughly. Add the cream and mix well together.

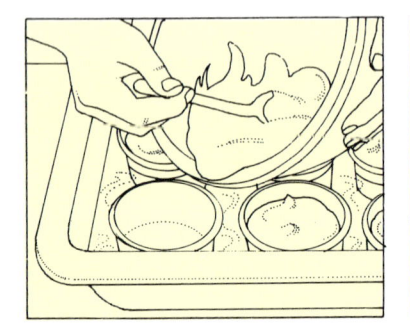

3 Stand six individual ramekin dishes in a roasting pan, then pour in enough hot water to come halfway up the sides of the dishes. Pour the custard mixture slowly into the ramekins, dividing it equally between them.

4 Bake in the oven at 300°F for about 1 hour or until set, then remove from pan and cool for 1 hour.

5 Refrigerate for 2–3 hours, preferably overnight. Sprinkle the top of each crème brûlée with the remaining sugar and put under a preheated hot broiler for 2–3 minutes until the sugar turns to caramel. Refrigerate again for 2–3 hours before serving.

CUSTARDS, SOUFFLÉS AND CREAMS

CRÊPES CREOLE

0.45* 🗋 $ $ ✱*

405–553 cals

* not including making the batter; freeze cooked crepes only

Serves 4–6

crêpe batter made with 1⅓ cups milk (see page 148)
finely grated rind and juice of 1 lime
¼ cup butter or margarine
½ cup light brown sugar
4 Tbsp dark rum
½ tsp ground cinnamon
3–4 bananas
orange and lime, to decorate

1 Make 8–12 crêpes in the usual way (see page 148). Slide each crepe out of the pan on to a warm plate and stack with wax paper in between.

2 Put the lime rind and juice in a saucepan with the butter, sugar, rum and cinnamon. Heat gently until the butter has melted and the sugar dissolved, stirring occasionally.

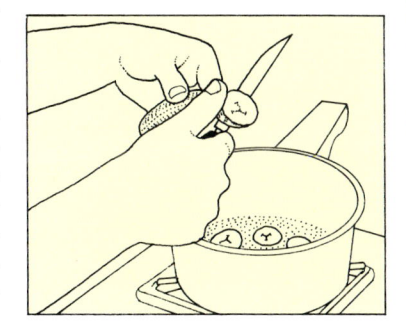

3 Peel the bananas and slice thinly into the sauce. Cook gently for 5 minutes until tender.

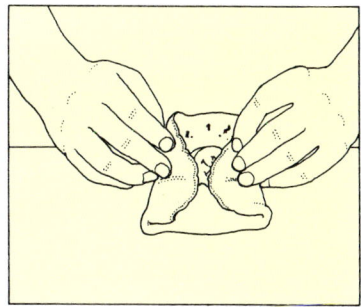

4 Remove the banana slices from the sauce with a slotted spoon. Place a few slices in the center of each crêpe, then fold the crêpes into envelopes around the cooked bananas.

5 Place in a warmed serving dish and pour over the hot sauce. Decorate with orange and lime twists and serve with cream, if liked.

RUM SOUFFLÉ OMELETTE

| 0.20 | 🍳 | $ $ | 513 cals |

Makes 1

2 eggs, separated
1 tsp sugar
1 Tbsp dark rum
1 Tbsp butter
1 Tbsp apricot jam, warmed
2 Tbsp confectioners sugar
hot metal skewers, to decorate (optional)

1 Put the egg yolks in a bowl with the sugar and rum. Mix well together.

2 Whisk the egg whites in a clean dry bowl until they are stiff and standing in peaks.

3 Melt the butter in a heavy-based omelette pan until foaming. Fold the egg whites quickly into the egg yolk mixture, then pour into the foaming butter.

4 Cook over moderate heat for 2–3 minutes until the underside of the omelette is golden brown, then place the pan under a preheated broiler and cook for a few minutes more until the top is golden brown.

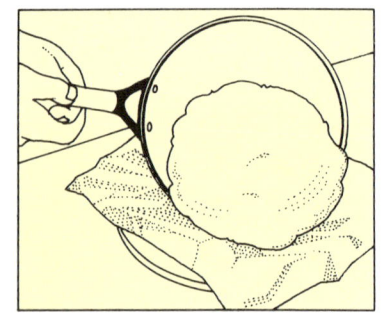

5 Slide the omelette on to a sheet of foil placed on a warmed serving plate. Spread with the warmed jam, then tip the foil to fold over the omelette.

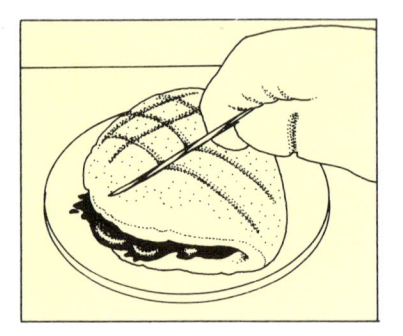

6 Sift the confectioners sugar thickly over the top of the omelette, then mark in a criss-cross pattern with hot metal skewers, if liked. Remove the foil and serve immediately.

OMELETTE PANS

A good-quality omelette pan is worth investing in if you want to make successful omelettes (both sweet and savory) every time. The pan should be heavy-based, ideally made from cast iron, copper or enamelled iron. The principle behind this is that the thickness of the base ensures that the egg cooks evenly. Special omelette pans are available, but a heavy-based frying pan with sloping sides and an easy-to-grip handle can be used with equal success.

For a perfect omelette, the egg mixture should not be more than $\frac{1}{4}$ inch thick, so for a 2- or 3-egg omelette you will need a 6–7 inch pan. If the mixture is too thin, the finished omelette will be dry and tough, if too thick, the outside will be overcooked before center is ready.

CUSTARDS, SOUFFLÉS AND CREAMS

IRRESISTIBLE DESSERTS

CUSTARDS, SOUFFLÉS AND CREAMS

FLOATING ISLANDS

0.50* | $ | 412 cals

*plus 1 hour chilling
Serves 4

5 egg yolks, beaten
2 cups milk
⅓ cup sugar plus 5 Tbsp
½ tsp vanilla extract
1 egg white

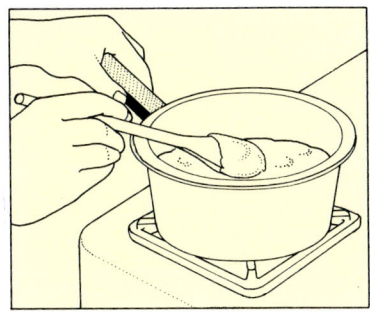

1 Make custard. Put egg yolks, milk, and ⅓ cup sugar in the top of a double boiler, or in a heavy-based saucepan over low heat. Cook gently for about 15 minutes, stirring constantly, until the mixture thickens and coats the back of the spoon. Stir in the vanilla extract.

2 Divide the custard between four stemmed glasses or dessert dishes. Cover and refrigerate for 1 hour.

3 Meanwhile, whisk the egg white until it will stand in stiff peaks. Add 2 Tbsp sugar and whisk again until the sugar is dissolved.

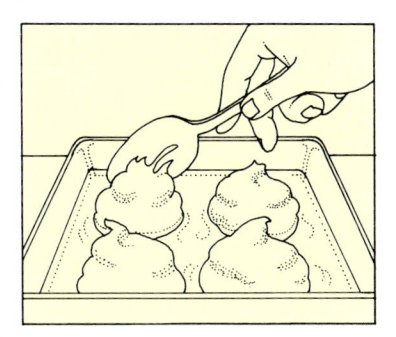

4 Put some cold water into a large skillet. Bring to a gentle simmer and spoon on the meringue in four even mounds. Poach for about 5 minutes until set, turning once.

5 Remove the meringues with a slotted spoon, drain for a minute on paper towels and spoon on to the custard in the stemmed glasses.

6 Put the remaining sugar into a heavy-based saucepan and cook, stirring constantly, for about 3 minutes or until it forms a golden syrup.

7 Remove from the heat and leave for 2 minutes to cool slightly, then drizzle a little of the warm syrup over the top of each meringue. Serve immediately.

IRRESISTIBLE DESSERTS

CUSTARDS, SOUFFLÉS AND CREAMS

Queen of Puddings

1.30 $ 306 cals

Serves 4

2 cups milk
2 Tbsp butter or margarine
finely grated rind of ½ a lemon
2 eggs, separated
⅓ cup sugar
1½ cups fresh white breadcrumbs
2 Tbsp red jam

1 Put the milk, butter and lemon rind in a saucepan and heat gently. Whisk the egg yolks and half of the sugar lightly and pour on the milk, stirring well.

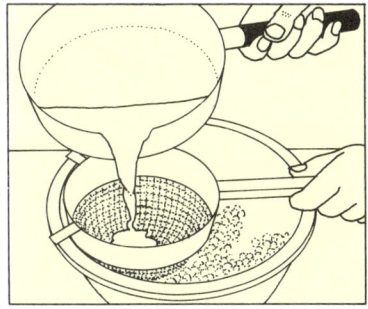

2 Strain the milk over the breadcrumbs. Pour into a greased 2 quart ovenproof dish and leave to stand for 15 minutes.

3 Bake in the oven at 350°F for 25–30 minutes, until lightly set; remove from the oven and set aside.

4 Put the jam in a small saucepan. Warm it over low heat, then spread it over the pudding.

5 Whisk the egg whites until stiff and add half the remaining sugar; whisk again and fold in the remaining sugar.

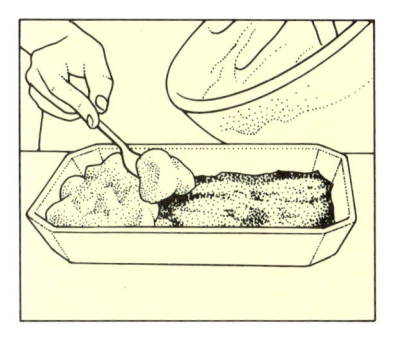

6 Pile the meringue on top of the jam and bake for a further 15–20 minutes, until the meringue is lightly browned.

QUEEN OF PUDDINGS

Queen of Puddings is a traditional English pudding from the nineteenth century. Original recipes for this homey dish used red jam and flavored the pudding with lemon rind, but you can make your own version according to what ingredients you have to hand. Any kind of jam can be used of course, or orange marmalade or ginger marmalade can be used instead of the jam, and grated orange rind or a little finely chopped stem ginger instead of the lemon. Lemon curd makes a delicious Queen of Puddings, with 2 Tbsp shredded coconut added to the breadcrumb and sugar mixture.

When finishing the pudding with the meringue topping, make absolutely sure that it covers the surface completely and that there are no gaps around the edges for the jam to seep through during baking. After piling the meringue on top, draw it up into peaks with the back of a metal spoon for an attractive effect. Better still, for a neater finish, pipe the meringue on top with a large star nozzle.

IRRESISTIBLE DESSERTS

Apple and Banana Fritters

1.00 $ 218–328 cals

Serves 4–6

¾ cup all-purpose flour
pinch of salt
6 Tbsp lukewarm water
4 tsp vegetable oil
2 egg whites
1 large cooking apple
2 bananas
juice of ½ a lemon
vegetable oil, for deep frying
sugar, to serve

1 Place the flour and salt into a bowl. Make a well in the center. Add the water and oil and beat to form a smooth batter.

2 Beat the egg whites in a clean dry bowl until they are stiff; then set aside.

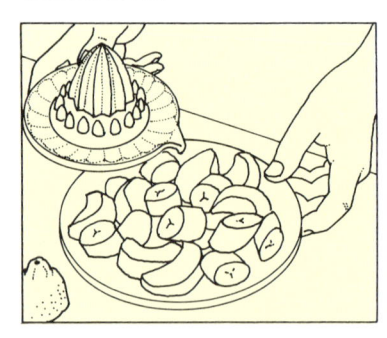

3 Peel, quarter and core the apple. Peel the bananas. Slice the fruit thickly and sprinkle at once with the lemon juice to prevent discoloration.

4 Fold the beaten egg whites into the batter, then immediately dip in the slices of fruit.

5 Deep-fry the fritters a few at a time in hot oil until puffed and light golden. Remove with a slotted spoon and pile on to a serving dish lined with paper towels. Serve immediately, sprinkled with sugar.

CUSTARDS, SOUFFLÉS AND CREAMS

Rum and Coffee Pudding

0.15* $ 283 cals

* plus 4 hours setting and 1 hour chilling

Serves 4

2½ cups plus 4 Tbsp milk
2 Tbsp sugar
2 tsp vegetable rennet powder
2 tsp rum
2 tsp instant coffee powder and chicory essence
⅔ cup sour cream
semisweet and white chocolate, to decorate

Note: Rennet powder is available at natural foods stores.

1 Put the 2½ cups milk in a saucepan and heat until just warm to the finger.

2 Add the sugar, rennet, rum and instant coffee powder and stir until the sugar has dissolved.

3 Pour the mixture at once into four individual dishes or a 4-cup shallow, edged serving dish. Put in a warm place, undisturbed, for 4 hours to set.

4 Lightly whisk the sour cream. Gradually add the 4 Tbsp milk, whisking until smooth.

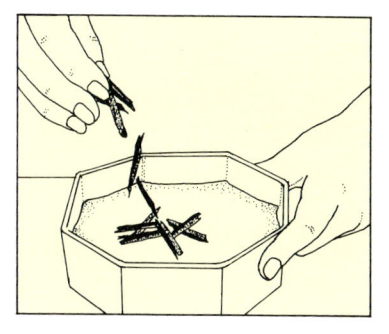

5 Carefully pour the sour cream mixture on top of the pudding with the coffee cream, taking care not to disturb the pudding. Decorate with coarsely grated chocolate. Refrigerate for 1 hour.

95

IRRESISTIBLE DESSERTS

CREMA FRITTA

1.25* | 314–471 cals

* plus 2–3 hours cooling

Serves 4–6

3 eggs
⅓ cup sugar
⅓ cup all-purpose flour
1 cup milk
1⅓ cups light cream
finely grated rind of ½ a lemon
2 cups dry white breadcrumbs
vegetable oil, for frying
sugar, to serve

1 In a large bowl, beat 2 eggs and the sugar together until the mixture is pale.

2 Add the flour, beating all the time, and then, very slowly, beat in the milk and cream. Add the lemon rind.

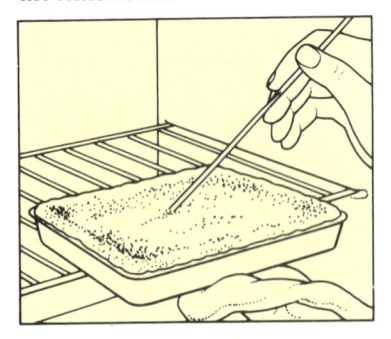

3 Pour the mixture into a buttered shallow 8-inch square cake pan. Bake in the oven at 350°F for about 1 hour, until a skewer inserted in the middle comes out clean. Leave to cool for 2–3 hours, preferably overnight.

4 When completely cold, cut into sixteen cubes and remove from the cake pan.

5 Beat the remaining egg in a bowl. Dip the cubes in the egg and then in the breadcrumbs until well coated.

6 Heat the oil in a frying pan and when hot, slide in the cubes. Fry for 2–3 minutes until golden brown and a crust is formed. Turn and fry the second side. Drain well on paper towels. Serve immediately, sprinkled with sugar.

CREMA FRITTA

Literally translated, this simple Italian dessert means "fried cream," which is in fact exactly what it is—a thick creamy sauce which is baked, chilled and cut into squares, then fried in oil until crisp and golden.

In Italy, it is traditional to celebrate *Carnevale*—the day before Lent—by eating *crema fritta*. Children and young people invite friends home and everyone eats *crema fritta* in the way that people in other countries eat crêpes. Sprinkled liberally with white sugar, they are always eaten informally—with the fingers.

CUSTARDS, SOUFFLÉS AND CREAMS

IRRESISTIBLE DESSERTS

CUSTARDS, SOUFFLÉS AND CREAMS

PRALINE ICE CREAM

0.50* $ $ ✱ 393 cals

* plus 45 minutes cooling, 9 hours freezing and 30 minutes softening

½ cup whole unblanched almonds
⅓ cup sugar
1⅓ cups milk
1 vanilla bean
1 egg
2 egg yolks
½ cup sugar
¾ cup whipping cream
coarsely grated semisweet chocolate, to decorate (optional)

1 Place the almonds and ⅓ cup sugar in a heavy-bottomed pan. Heat slowly until the sugar caramelizes, turning occasionally.

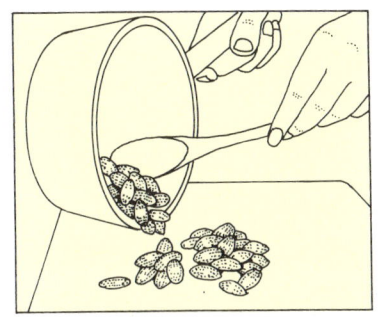

2 Pour the mixture on to an oiled baking sheet to cool and harden for about 15 minutes.

3 Use a mouli grater, blender or food processor to grind the cooled praline to a powder.

4 Bring the milk and vanilla bean to the boil, take off the heat and leave to infuse for 15 minutes.

5 Beat the egg, egg yolks, and ½ cup sugar until pale in color, strain in the milk, stir, and return to the saucepan. Cook slowly for about 10 minutes until the custard coats the back of a wooden spoon—do not boil. Cool completely for 30–40 minutes. Lightly whip the cream and fold into the custard.

6 Freeze the mixture for about 3 hours until mushy. Beat well, then fold in the praline powder. Spoon into a freezer container and freeze for about 6 hours until firm.

7 Transfer to the refrigerator to soften for 30 minutes before serving. Serve scooped into glasses and decorated with coarsely grated chocolate, if liked.

PRALINE

Praline is a French confection made by cooking almonds and sugar together until the sugar caramelizes, then crushing the set mixture to a powder. This recipe for Praline Ice Cream uses brown praline, although white praline can also be used.

White praline has a milder flavor than brown; they are both made in exactly the same way, the only difference is that for brown praline almonds in their skins are used, whereas white praline uses blanched almonds.

IRRESISTIBLE DESSERTS

Frozen Brandy Creams

| 0.30* | 🍳 | $ $ | ❄ | 423 cals |

* plus 30 minutes cooling and 5 hours freezing

Serves 4

4 egg yolks

¾ cup sugar

6 Tbsp brandy

⅔ cup whipping cream

chocolate coffee beans, to decorate

1 Place the egg yolks, sugar and brandy in a deep, medium-sized heatproof bowl. Using a wooden spoon, stir well.

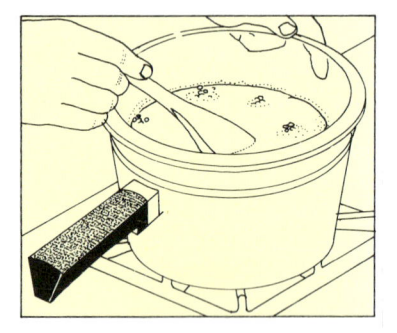

2 Place the bowl over a pan of simmering water; the bowl base should not touch the water. Stir the mixture all the time for about 15 minutes, until it thickens slightly and will just coat the back of the spoon. Do not overheat or the eggs may curdle. Take off heat and cool for 30 minutes.

3 Lightly whip the cream and stir half into the cold brandy mixture. Pour into four small soufflé or ramekin dishes. Freeze for at least 5 hours, until firm.

4 To serve, decorate each ramekin with a whirl of the remaining whipped cream, then top with a chocolate coffee bean. Serve immediately.

CUSTARDS, SOUFFLÉS AND CREAMS

IRRESISTIBLE DESSERTS

TEA CREAM

0.45* $ $ 293 cals

* plus 2–3 hours setting

Serves 4

1⅓ cups milk
1 Earl Grey tea bag
2 eggs, separated
2 Tbsp sugar
3 Tbsp water
3 tsp gelatine
⅔ cup whipping cream

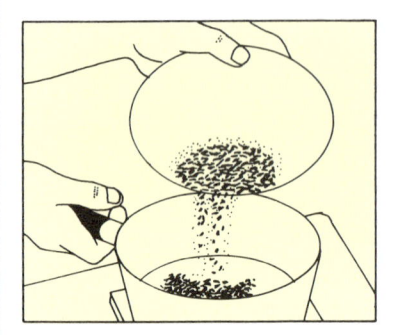

1 Put the milk into a saucepan, add the tea and bring to the boil. Remove from the heat and leave to infuse for 10–15 minutes, or until the milk is well colored with the tea.

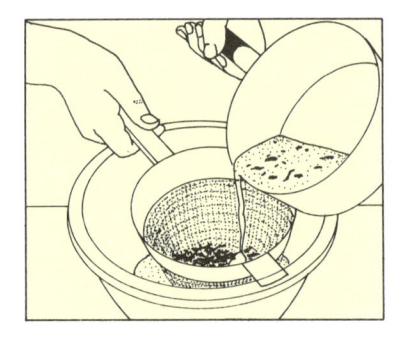

2 Beat the egg yolks with the sugar, then strain on the milk and mix well. Return to the pan and cook gently for 10 minutes, stirring all the time, until the custard thickens slightly and just coats the back of the spoon.

3 Put the water in a small heat-proof bowl and sprinkle in the gelatine. Stand the bowl over a saucepan of hot water and heat gently until dissolved. Mix into the tea mixture, then leave for about 2 hours until beginning to set. Stir the mixture occasionally.

4 Whip the cream until thick but not stiff, then fold into the custard. Finally, whisk the egg whites until stiff and fold into the mixture.

5 Pour the cream mixture into a dampened 4-cup mold and refrigerate for about 2–3 hours until set. Turn out on to a chilled dish to serve.

TEA CREAM

Earl Grey tea, a blended black tea flavored with bergamot oil, gives this unusual tea cream a subtle, perfumed flavor.

It isn't essential to use Earl Grey, however; you can use any of your favorite Ceylon or China teas, although aromatic teas are more flavorsome in cooking. Why not try jasmine tea, lapsang souchong, or orange pekoe?

CUSTARDS, SOUFFLÉS AND CREAMS

IRRESISTIBLE DESSERTS

CUSTARDS, SOUFFLÉS AND CREAMS

Tutti Frutti Ice Cream

0.45* | $ $ | ✳ | 475–593 cals

* plus 2–3 hours soaking, 30 minutes cooling and 5 hours freezing

Serves 8–10

6 Tbsp dark rum
⅓ cup light raisins
⅓ cup pitted dates
⅓ cup glacé cherries
⅓ cup dried apricots
2½ cups milk
1 vanilla bean or a few drops of vanilla extract
6 egg yolks
1 cup sugar
2⅔ cups whipping cream

1 Pour the rum into a screw-top jar or a bowl. Add the raisins, then roughly snip the dates, cherries and apricots into the jar or bowl. Make sure all the fruit is coated with rum. Cover and leave to macerate for 2–3 hours shaking or tossing occasionally until the rum is absorbed.

2 Meanwhile, make the ice cream. Put the milk and vanilla bean or extract into a heavy-based saucepan and bring almost to the boil. Remove from the heat, cover and leave to infuse for 15 minutes.

3 Beat the egg yolks and sugar together in a bowl until thick and pale, stir in the milk and strain back into the saucepan.

4 Cook the custard gently over a low heat, stirring all the time, until it coats the back of a wooden spoon. Do not boil or it will curdle. Cover and leave the custard for about 30 minutes until completely cold.

5 Pour into a chilled, shallow freezer container and freeze for about 2 hours until mushy.

6 Turn the frozen mixture into a large, chilled bowl and mash with a whisk or fork.

7 Lightly whip the cream and fold into the mixture with the macerated fruit. Return to the freezer and freeze for 3 hours, or until required, until firm.

8 Allow to soften for about 30 minutes in the refrigerator before serving.

IRRESISTIBLE DESSERTS

Fruit Desserts

There's nothing to compare with fresh fruits for making delicious desserts in next to no time. The beautiful colors of fresh fruit such as oranges, apples, peaches, raspberries, and strawberries attract the eye and titillate the palate—even with those who say they don't have a sweet tooth. It's the natural sweet simplicity of a fresh fruit dessert that's far more appealing—and satisfying—than any elaborate concoction.

FRUIT DESSERTS

ORANGES IN CARAMEL

0.30* | $ | 155–310 cals

* plus 2–3 hours chilling

Serves 4–8

8 medium juicy oranges
1⅓ cups sugar
2 Tbsp orange-flavored liqueur

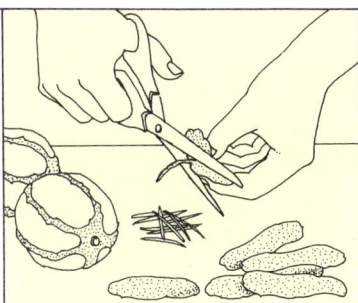

1 Thinly pare the rind from 2 oranges, keeping it free of white pith. Cut the rind into very thin julienne strips with scissors or a sharp knife. Place in a small saucepan and cover well with water. Cover the pan and cook for 5 minutes until the rind is tender. Drain and rinse under cold running water.

2 Cut away all the pith from these oranges and both rind and pith from the remaining oranges. (Reserve any juice that may be squeezed out from the oranges as you do this.)

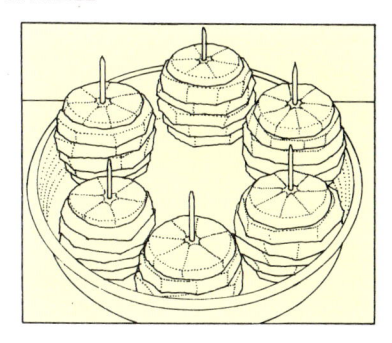

3 Slice the orange flesh into rounds, discarding any seeds, and arrange in a serving dish. If liked, the orange rounds can be re-assembled in the shape of the orange. Secure each with a wooden toothpick then arrange in the serving dish.

4 Place the sugar and 1⅓ cups water in a saucepan and heat gently until the sugar has dissolved. Bring to the boil and boil until caramel colored. Remove the pan from the heat, add 3 Tbsp water and return it to a low heat to dissolve the caramel. Add the reserved orange juice and the liqueur.

5 Leave the caramel syrup to cool for 2–3 minutes, then pour over the oranges. Top with the julienne strips. Refrigerate for 2–3 hours, turning the oranges occasionally, before serving.

--- VARIATIONS ---

For a sweet, crunchy topping to this classic orange dessert, make caramel chips: dissolve ½ cup sugar very gently in ⅓ cup water. Increase the heat and boil rapidly without stirring until the syrup turns a rich-brown caramel color. Pour at once into a greased shallow jelly roll pan, then leave until cold and set. Crush with a mallet or rolling pin into fine pieces and sprinkle over the oranges just before serving (not before or the caramel will go soft).

IRRESISTIBLE DESSERTS

BAKED CHERRIES

1.00* ✳ 449–674 cals

* plus 30 minutes chilling

Serves 4–6

1½ lb fresh red or black cherries
⅔ cup sugar
2 Tbsp all-purpose flour
1 Tbsp water
1 tsp kirsch (optional)
shortcrust pastry (see page 152) for 8-inch pie
sugar, to serve

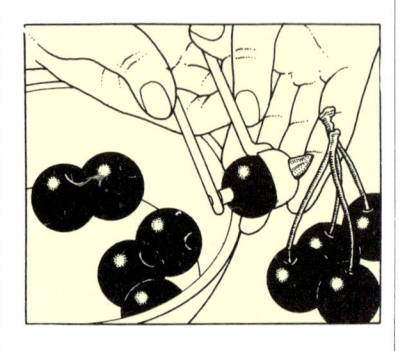

1 Pit the cherries, but keep them as whole as possible. Then mix the sugar and flour together and layer the cherries and sugar mixture in an 8-inch deep dish pie pan. Sprinkle over the water and kirsch, if using.

2 Roll out the pastry on a floured work surface to a shape 2 inches wider than the pie pan. Dampen the rim of the pie pan, then cut a 1-inch strip from the outer edge of the pastry and press on to the rim. Dampen the pastry rim and cover with pastry lid, sealing edges well. Use the pastry trimmings to decorate. Chill for 30 minutes.

3 Make a hole in the center of the pastry. Bake in the oven at 400°F for 25–30 minutes until the pastry is lightly browned and the fruit is cooked. Sprinkle immediately with sugar and serve warm.

TARTE TATIN

1.00* $ ✳ 379 cals

* plus 30 minutes chilling

Serves 8

½ cup plus 2 Tbsp butter or margarine
1¼ cups all-purpose flour
⅓ cup plus 1 Tbsp sugar
1 egg yolk
1 Tbsp water
1 lb crisp eating apples
whipped cream, to serve

1 Cut ½ cup butter into the flour until the mixture resembles fine cornmeal. Add 1 Tbsp sugar. Blend the egg yolk with the water and stir into the mixture. Knead the dough lightly, then refrigerate while making the filling.

2 In a saucepan, melt the remaining butter and add the remaining sugar. Heat until caramelized and golden brown. Remove from the heat and pour into an 8-inch round cake pan.

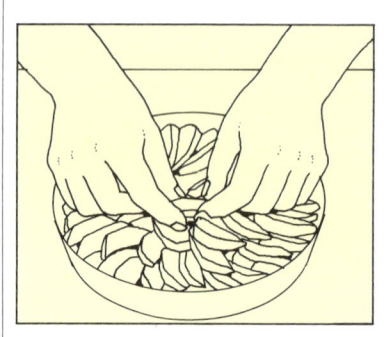

3 Peel, core and halve the apples and slice them into ½-inch pieces. Pack them tightly to fill the bottom of the pan, leaving no gaps.

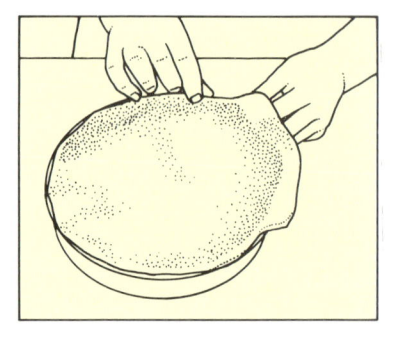

4 Roll out the pastry on a floured work surface to a round slightly larger than the pan. Place on top of the apples and tuck in around the edges of the tin. Refrigerate for 30 minutes.

5 Bake in the oven at 400°F for 30–35 minutes until the pastry is golden. Turn out, apple side uppermost, on to a serving dish. Serve hot, with a bowl of whipped cream.

TARTE TATIN

Correctly called *Tarte des Demoiselles Tatin* in French, this famous upside-down apple tart is named after the sisters Tatin, hoteliers in the nineteenth century who originated the recipe.

There are now numerous versions of the original recipe, which has become something of a classic in French cookery. Most recipes use shortcrust pastry as here, although some use puff, but in all versions the pastry is baked on the top so that the apples are completely sealed in with their juices, then the tart turned out upside down for serving. In France, *crème fraîche* is usually served with warm tarte Tatin; it is slightly more acidic than our fresh cream, which makes a good contrast with the sweetness of the caramelized apples. Alternatively, serve with cream.

FRUIT DESSERTS

IRRESISTIBLE DESSERTS

Rhubarb and Orange Chiffon Pie

0.45* | $ | ✳ | 589 cals

* plus 1 hour cooling and at least 2 hours chilling

Serves 4

1½ cups graham cracker crumbs
⅓ cup light brown sugar
6 Tbsp unsalted butter, melted
1 lb 4-oz can rhubarb, drained
finely grated rind and juice of 1 large orange
2 eggs, separated
½ cup sugar
2 Tbsp cornstarch
½ tsp ground ginger
orange slices, to decorate

1 In a bowl, mix together the graham cracker crumbs and light brown sugar, then stir in the melted unsalted butter.

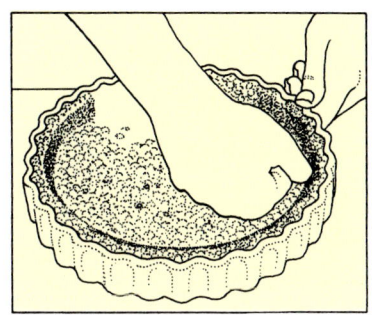

2 Press the mixture over the base and sides of a 8-inch fluted tart pan. Chill in the refrigerator while preparing the filling.

3 Work the rhubarb to a purée in an electric blender. Put the orange rind and juice into a heavy-based saucepan. Add the egg yolks, sugar, cornstarch and ground ginger. Heat gently, stirring constantly, until thick. Stir into the rhubarb purée.

4 Whisk the egg whites until stiff. Fold into the rhubarb custard, then spoon the mixture into the crust. Refrigerate for at least 4 hours, or overnight. Decorate with orange slices just before serving.

IRRESISTIBLE DESSERTS

RØDGRØD

| 0.35* | $ | ✽ | 339–452 cals |

* plus 10 minutes cooling and 30 minutes chilling

Serves 6–8

1 lb fresh red currants

1 lb fresh raspberries or 1 package frozen, thawed

3 Tbsp arrowroot

1⅓ to 3 cups sugar, if using fresh fruit

¼ cup blanched slivered almonds and whipped cream, to decorate

1 Place the fresh fruits in a saucepan with 4 Tbsp water. Simmer gently for about 20 minutes or until really soft.

2 Purée in a blender or food processor until smooth, then strain. If using canned fruit, strain.

3 Blend a little of the purée with the arrowroot, put the rest into a saucepan and bring slowly to boiling point. Stir into the blended mixture, then return it all to the pan. Bring to the boil again, cook for 2–3 minutes and sweeten to taste if using fresh fruit. Leave to cool for 10 minutes.

4 Toast almonds lightly under the broiler. Cool for 5 minutes.

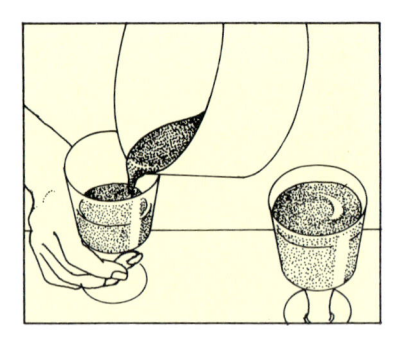

5 Pour the rødgrød into individual tall or shallow glasses and refrigerate for 30 minutes. Top with whipped cream and the almonds just before serving.

RØDGRØD

Rødgrød is a Danish dessert which is best described as a fruit soup. It is always made with fresh soft summer fruit: red currants and raspberries are used in our version, although black currants, blackberries, strawberries, cherries and even rhubarb can be used, depending on what is available. The important thing is to mix at least two of these fruits together to provide good flavor and color.

Such fruit soups are popular all over Scandinavia, and are sometimes even eaten as an appetizer, either hot or cold. In Finland, they are called *kiisseli*, and are often made with more unusual soft red fruits such as bilberries, cloudberries and cranberries.

This recipe for rødgrød is refreshingly simple, whereas some recipes use spices such as cinnamon and the thinly pared zest of citrus fruit—you can add these too if you wish. Fresh whipped cream to serve is traditional, or you can use sour cream or natural yogurt, in which case the soup will look most attractive if the cream or yogurt is swirled over the top just before serving.

FRUIT DESSERTS

IRRESISTIBLE DESSERTS

FRUIT DESSERTS

POIRES BELLE HÉLÈNE

| 2.00 | 🍳 | $ $ | 357 cals |

$\frac{2}{3}$ cup sugar
$3\frac{3}{4}$ cups water
thinly pared rind and juice of 2 oranges
6 pears (preferably Bosc)
8 oz semisweet chocolate, broken into pieces
4 Tbsp orange-flavored liqueur
orange slices, to decorate

1. Put the sugar, water and half the orange rind in a large heavy-based saucepan and heat gently, without stirring, until the sugar has dissolved.

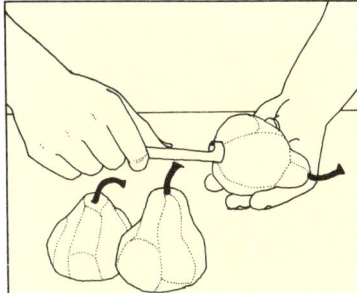

2. Meanwhile, peel the pears quickly (to prevent discoloration), leaving the stalks on. Cut out the cores from the bottom and level them so that the pears will stand upright.

3. Stand the pears in the syrup, cover the pan and simmer gently for 20 minutes or until tender. Remove from the heat and leave to cool, covered tightly. Spoon the syrup over the pears occasionally during cooling.

4. Meanwhile, make the decoration. Cut the remaining orange rind into thin matchstick (julienne) strips. Blanch in boiling water for 2 minutes, then drain and immediately refresh under cold running water. Leave to drain on paper towels.

5. Make the chocolate sauce. Put the chocolate and liqueur in a heatproof bowl standing over a pan of gently simmering water. Heat gently until chocolate melts.

6. Remove the pears from the syrup, stand on a large serving dish, or 6 individual dishes and chill for 2 hours. Discard the orange rind from the syrup. Stir the melted chocolate into $\frac{2}{3}$ cup of the syrup with the orange juice, then slowly bring to the boil, stirring constantly. Simmer, stirring, until the sauce is thick and syrupy.

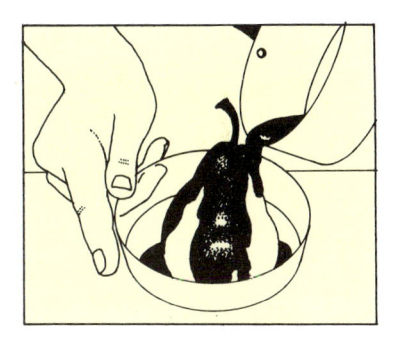

7. To serve, pour the hot chocolate sauce over the cold pears and sprinkle with the orange julienne. Decorate with orange slices and serve immediately.

IRRESISTIBLE DESSERTS

Citrus Soufflé

1.30* | $ $ ✳ | 290–386 cals

* plus 4 hours setting

Serves 6–8

| finely grated rind and juice of 1 lemon |
| finely grated rind and juice of 1 orange |
| juice of 1 grapefruit |
| 3 tsp gelatine |
| 4 eggs, separated |
| ⅔ cup sugar |
| 1⅓ cups whipping cream |
| crushed sugar cookies and candied oranges and lemons, to decorate |

1 Prepare a 6-inch soufflé dish. Cut a double thickness of parchment paper long enough to go around the outside of the dish and 2–3 inches deeper. Secure around the outside with paper clips and string.

2 Pour the fruit juices into a heatproof bowl and sprinkle in the gelatine. Stand the bowl over a saucepan of hot water and heat gently until dissolved. Remove the bowl from the water and set aside to cool for 45 minutes.

3 Put the fruit rinds, egg yolks and sugar in a large heatproof bowl and stand over the pan of gently simmering water. Whisk until the mixture is thick and holds a ribbon trail.

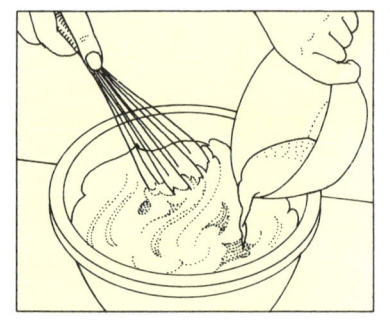

4 Remove the bowl from the pan and whisk in the gelatine liquid. Leave until beginning to set, whisking occasionally.

5 Whip the cream until it will stand in soft peaks. Whisk the egg whites until stiff. Fold the cream into the soufflé, then the egg whites, until evenly blended.

6 Pour the mixture into the prepared soufflé dish and level the surface. Chill in the refrigerator for at least 4 hours until set.

7 Carefully remove the paper from the edge of the soufflé. Press the crushed sugar cookies around the exposed edge, then decorate the top with candied fruit. Serve chilled.

VARIATIONS

Children love the tangy flavor of this soufflé, and if you don't want to go to the trouble of preparing a soufflé dish with a collar, it can be set in a serving bowl like a mousse. Vary the flavor of this soufflé according to the fruit available—make it with just oranges and lemons if you like, or with just one citrus fruit. For an extra special dinner party, add a spoonful or two of orange-flavored liqueur.

FRUIT DESSERTS

IRRESISTIBLE DESSERTS

BRANDIED STUFFED APRICOTS

0.35* | $ | 274 cals

* plus 50 minutes cooling and 2–3 hours chilling

Serves 4

16 small apricots
8 Tbsp apricot brandy
2 Tbsp sugar
finely grated rind and juice of 1 lemon
$\frac{2}{3}$ cup water
$1\frac{1}{4}$ cups cottage cheese
$\frac{1}{4}$ cup cream cheese
1 Tbsp confectioners sugar, sifted
chopped toasted hazelnuts, to decorate

1 Place the apricots in a saucepan with the brandy, sugar, 1 Tbsp lemon juice, and the water. Poach gently for about 15 minutes until just tender. Remove apricots and leave to cool for 30 minutes.

2 Bring the poaching liquid to the boil, bubble for 2–3 minutes until well reduced and syrupy. Leave to cool for 20 minutes.

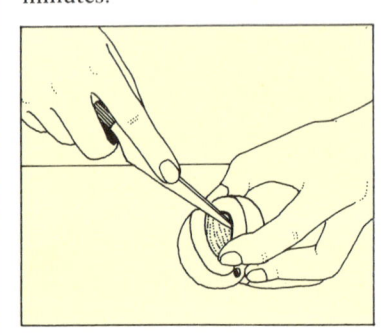

3 Using a sharp knife, skin the apricots. Slice almost in half and remove the pit.

4 Sieve the cottage cheese into a bowl, add the cream cheese, confectioners sugar and grated lemon rind and beat together until well mixed.

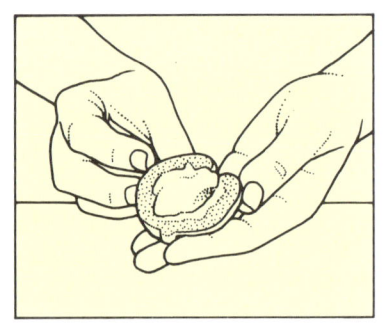

5 Sandwich the apricots together with a little of the cheese mixture. Divide the apricots between four individual glass dishes.

6 Spoon a little of the cooled syrup over the apricots, then sprinkle with chopped nuts. Refrigerate for 2–3 hours before serving.

APRICOTS

Apricots originated in China, but are now grown all over the world, wherever the weather is kind enough to ripen this delicate fruit. Smaller and more unusual than its relatives the nectarine and peach, the apricot is highly prized for its unique flavor and aroma. Fresh apricots do not keep well, however, and their season is relatively short compared to other fruits. Most apricots are used for canning and drying or for jam making and preserves.

If fresh apricots are not available, this recipe can be made with small peaches or nectarines, but as these are always larger than apricots you will only need half the quantity, thus allowing two fruits per person. Ordinary brandy can be substituted for apricot or peach brandy.

FRUIT DESSERTS

IRRESISTIBLE DESSERTS

PINEAPPLE AND BANANA FLAMBÉ

0.50 | $ $ | 235–313 cals

Serves 6–8

1 medium pineapple
2 lb firm bananas
1 cup dried figs
¼ cup butter or margarine
⅔ cup light brown sugar
3 Tbsp lemon juice
½ tsp ground allspice
4 Tbsp dark rum

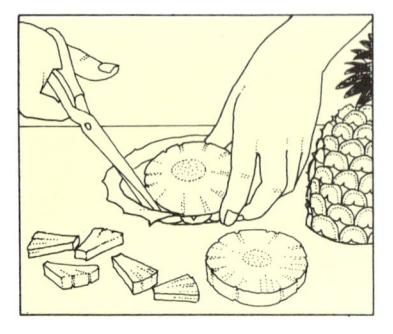

1. Slice the pineapple into ½-inch pieces. Snip off the skin and cut the flesh into chunks, discarding the core.

2. Peel and thickly slice the bananas into the bottom of a shallow ovenproof dish; spoon the pineapple on top.

3. Cut the figs into coarse shreds and scatter over the fruit. Then put the butter, sugar, strained lemon juice and spice together in a saucepan and heat until well blended; pour over the prepared fruit.

4. Cover tightly and bake in the oven at 400°F for 25 minutes until the fruit is tender.

5. Heat the rum gently in a small saucepan, remove from the heat and ignite with a match. Pour immediately over the fruit and bring the dish to the table while still flaming.

SERVING IDEA

For a special occasion such as a dinner party, you can serve this dessert in the pineapple shells. It will look really spectacular if carried flaming to the table, and any mixture which will not fit into the pineapple shells can be served separately in a fruit bowl.

To make two pineapple shells from one pineapple: with a large, sharp knife, slice the pineapple in half lengthways, cutting right through the crown and base. Insert the blade of a long, serrated knife into the flesh of one pineapple half, about ¼ inch in from the edge of the shell, and cut all around the inside. Cut through the flesh in parallel lines, first lengthways and then crossways to produce squares of flesh (take care not to cut through the skin at the base). Scoop out the flesh with a sharp-edged teaspoon. Repeat with the second pineapple half, then turn both shells upside-down and leave to drain before filling.

FRUIT DESSERTS

Raspberry Parfait

0.30* $ $ 351 cals

* plus 2–3 hours freezing and 30 minutes softening

| 1 lb fresh raspberries, hulled |
| 1 cup confectioners sugar, sifted |
| ½ cup sugar |
| ⅓ cup water |
| 2 egg whites |
| 1 Tbsp kirsch or raspberry-flavored liqueur (optional) |
| squeeze of lemon juice |
| 1⅓ cups whipping cream |
| fresh mint leaves, to decorate |

1 Purée the raspberries in a blender or food processor, then strain to remove the seeds. Stir confectioners sugar into purée.

2 Put the sugar and water into a heavy-based saucepan and dissolve over gentle heat.

3 When dissolved, bring to boil and boil until syrupy. Remove from the heat.

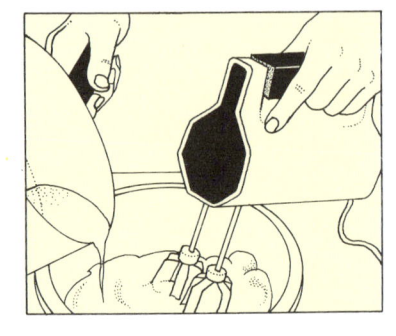

4 Whisk the egg whites until very stiff, then pour the hot sugar syrup on to them, whisking until thick, shiny and mousse-like. Leave for 10 minutes until cool.

FRUIT DESSERTS

5 Flavor the raspberry purée with the liqueur, if using, and the lemon juice. Fold into the meringue mixture.

6 Lightly whip the cream and fold into the raspberry mixture. Taste for sweetness and add more sugar if necessary. Pour into a chilled shallow freezer container and freeze for 3–4 hours until the mixture is firm.

7 Allow the raspberry parfait to soften for 30 minutes in the refrigerator before serving. Decorate with the mint leaves.

KIWI FRUIT SORBET

0.30* | $ | ✳ | 103 cals

* plus 30 minutes cooling and 6 hours freezing

$\frac{1}{3}$ cup sugar
$\frac{2}{3}$ cup water
6 kiwi fruit
2 egg whites
slices of kiwi fruit, to decorate
orange-flavored liqueur and sugar cookies, to serve

1 Place the sugar in saucepan with the water. Heat gently until the sugar dissolves, then simmer for 2 minutes. Cool for 30 minutes.

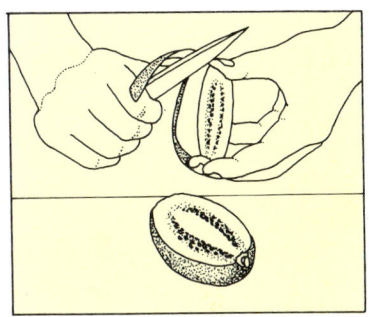

2 Halve the kiwi fruit and peel thinly or pull away the skins without damaging the flesh.

3 Place the fruit in a blender or food processor with the cool syrup. Work to a smooth purée, then sieve to remove the seeds. Pour into a chilled shallow freezer container. Freeze for 2 hours until mushy.

4 Beat the mixture with a fork to break down any ice crystals.

5 Whisk the egg whites until stiff, then fold into the fruit mixture until evenly blended. Return to freezer for 4 hours.

6 Scoop into individual glass dishes, decorate and spoon over some liqueur. Serve with sugar cookies.

IRRESISTIBLE DESSERTS

FRUIT DESSERTS

FRUDITÉS

| 0.20 | $ $ | 245 cals |

$\frac{2}{3}$ cup whipping cream
$\frac{2}{3}$ cup sour cream
2 Tbsp confectioners sugar, sifted
$\frac{1}{2}$ lb apricots
$\frac{1}{2}$ lb strawberries
$\frac{1}{3}$ lb black or green grapes
2 crisp eating apples
2 bananas
juice of 1 lemon

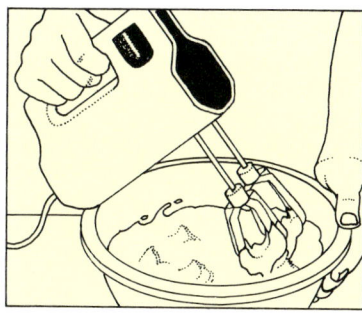

1 First prepare the dip. Whip the two creams together with the confectioners sugar until standing in soft peaks. Pipe or spoon into six individual dishes.

2 Prepare the fruit. Halve and pit the apricots. Wash the strawberries under cold running water, but do not hull them.

3 Halve the grapes if they are not the seedless variety and flick out the seeds.

4 Quarter and core the apples, but do not peel them. Peel the bananas and cut into 1$\frac{1}{2}$-inch chunks.

5 Arrange the fruit on individual serving plates and sprinkle immediately with lemon juice to prevent discoloration.

6 Place the dishes of cream dip next to the fruit and serve immediately. Use fingers or small fondue forks to dunk the fruit into the cream dip.

FRUDITÉS

This is a sweet version of the French starter *crudités* which consists of fresh raw vegetables served with a vinaigrette dressing or mayonnaise-type dip. Instead of vegetables, frudités uses raw fresh fruit served with a sweet creamy dip! And it's as much fun for your guests as a fondue party if you provide forks for dipping the fruit into the dressing. Frudités can be made at any time of year, with whatever fruit happens to be in season. As long as the fruit is in peak condition and the combination of different types interesting, the dish is bound to be a success.

In the winter, when fruit is scarce and more expensive, you can cut up squares of plain cake, such as pound cake or sponge cake. And if you are entertaining children amongst your guests, they would appreciate a chocolate sauce to dip their fruit into—either make a hot chocolate sauce as you would use for ice cream, or use a commercial variety if time is short.

IRRESISTIBLE DESSERTS

Mandarin and Lychee Mousse

0.45* | $ | ✳ | 292 cals

* plus 30 minutes cooling and at least 2 hours setting

3 eggs, separated
2 egg yolks
½ cup sugar
10½-oz can mandarin oranges in natural juice
11-oz can lychees in syrup
3 tsp gelatine
⅔ cup whipping cream

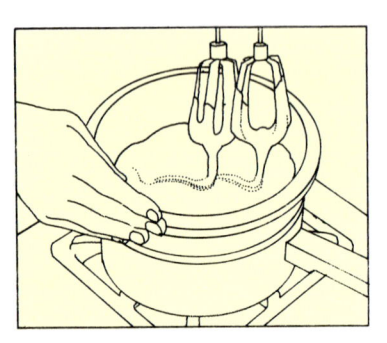

1 Put the 5 egg yolks and sugar in a large heatproof bowl and stand over a saucepan of gently simmering water. Whisk until the mixture is thick and holds a ribbon trail, then remove the bowl from the pan. Leave for 30 minutes, whisking occasionally.

2 Reserve 4 Tbsp of the mandarin juice. Purée half the oranges and the remaining juice in a blender or food processor with the lychees and half the syrup.

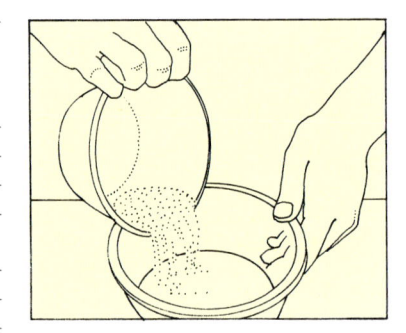

3 Put the reserved mandarin syrup in a heatproof bowl and sprinkle in the gelatine. Stand the bowl over a saucepan of hot water and heat gently until dissolved. Remove the bowl from the pan and leave to cool slightly.

4 Stir the mandarin purée into the cooled egg yolk mixture, then stir in the gelatine liquid until evenly mixed.

5 Whip the cream until standing in soft peaks. Whisk the egg whites until stiff. Fold first the cream and then the egg whites into the mousse until evenly blended. Turn into a glass serving bowl and chill for at least 2 hours until set.

6 When the mousse is set serve decorated with the reserved mandarin oranges and extra whipped cream, if liked.

LYCHEES
The tree fruit lychee (lichee or litchi as it is also known) originated in China, but it is now grown in tropical countries elsewhere in the world. Canned peeled lychees, with their translucent white flesh, are readily available. The skin of a lychee is a most attractive reddish brown with a rough almost brittle texture, but the fresh fruit is rarely seen outside specialty markets. The unique perfumed flavor of lychees, and their beautifully smooth texture, makes them an interesting ingredient to include in a mousse such as the one on this page.

FRUIT DESSERTS

IRRESISTIBLE DESSERTS

PRUNE AND PORT CREAM

| 0.45* | $ | ✱ | 433 cals |

* plus overnight soaking and 2 hours chilling

Serves 4

1 cup pitted prunes, soaked overnight in cold water
$\frac{1}{3}$ cup sugar
4 Tbsp port
finely grated rind and juice of 1 medium orange
$\frac{2}{3}$ cup thick custard, cooled
$\frac{2}{3}$ cup whipping cream
cookies, to serve

1 Drain the prunes, then put in a saucepan with the sugar, port, orange rind and juice. Simmer for about 15 minutes until soft. Leave to cool slightly, then purée in a blender or food processor. Leave to cool completely.

2 Fold the cooled custard into the puréed prunes. Whip the cream until it will stand in soft peaks, then fold into the prune custard until evenly blended.

3 Divide the mixture between four individual glasses, then chill in the refrigerator for about 2 hours until firm. Serve chilled, with cookies.

Useful Information
and
Basic Recipes

Basic Equipment

Whether making an elaborate dessert for a dinner party, or whipping up a simple pudding to end a family meal, having the right equipment is all-important. Not only will it make your task much easier, but it will also greatly improve the results, in terms of both flavor and appearance — many desserts, for example, can be made in attractive molds and then turned out, to offer pretty and unusual shapes.

BASIC EQUIPMENT

Most desserts and puddings can be made without anything other than good basic kitchen equipment. However, there are a number of pans and dishes which will help make desserts look more attractive and be more authentic.

Pans and dishes come in different materials. Good-quality pans should last a lifetime if treated with care. Aluminum pans are excellent for baking as the metal is a good conductor of heat; pans with non-stick surfaces are easily cleaned. Ceramic dishes are good for puddings and pies which must be served straight from the oven. Thick ceramic dishes are also good when baking slowly such as with custards. Pans with removable bases make it easier to remove the pastry or cake.

Use the size of pan specified in the recipe. Too large a pan and the mixture may cook too quickly or it may not rise properly. On the other hand, if the pan is too small the mixture may not cook evenly and will produce an uneven texture and an over browned surface. If necessary use a pan which is too large rather than too small and reduce the cooking time by about 5–10 minutes. Chilled desserts made in the wrong pan size may look misshapen and out of proportion.

MOLDS AND BOWLS

Pudding molds come in a range of sizes and are made of tough porcelain which won't crack even in the pressure cooker. The steep tapered sides help the pudding keep its shape when turned out.

Stainless steel bowls are ideal for small jobs like melting chocolate over hot water, whisking egg whites and whipping cream. A *copper bowl* is only used for whisking egg whites and may be worth buying — they are expensive — if you make a lot of meringues, but the bowl requires special care.

Dessert molds have sloping sides which help to make turning out gelatines and mousses easier than if the dish had straight sides. Molds for foods which are chilled or frozen are best made of thin metal which helps speed up chilling time.

A *charlotte mold* is a large round mold with sloping sides and is

A selection of pudding and dessert molds

BASIC EQUIPMENT

A selection of baking dishes and flan, tart and pie pans

used for making the classic charlotte russe. *Decorative molds* can make gelatines and mousses look especially attractive. These molds come in tall, flat, funneled or tubular shapes. Individual-sized decorative molds are also available. *Bombe molds* are curved and come with a lid. *China molds* are used for cornstarch-thickened puddings as metal can sometimes tinge the color of a milk-based pudding.

How long a pudding takes to set in a mold largely depends on its size. If using individual-sized molds instead of one large mold setting times can be shortened by as much as 2 hours.

To prepare a mold for a chilled dessert rinse it under cold running water and keep the wetted mold in the refrigerator until the mixture is ready for it.

BAKING DISHES

A *soufflé dish* has straight sides to allow the greatest height when the soufflé mixture rises in the oven. It can be made of porcelain, earthenware or glass and comes in a range of sizes. Soufflé dishes are also useful for making mousses and baked custards. Individual-sized soufflé dishes are often used for baking instead of *ramekins*, which are slope-sided dishes used for crème caramel. Little *custard pots* are used for making *petits pots de chocolats*.

A *spring-release pan* has a side section which can be removed without disturbing the base. These often come with alternative bases. Cheesecakes are usually baked or chilled in these pans.

FLUTED TART AND PIE PANS

Fluted tart pans may come with a removable base. These are primarily used for fruit tarts.

Pie pans are shallow, round dishes made of metal, oven-tempered glass or ceramic; they are used for the traditional single or double crust pies.

Individual tarts are made in sheets of *tartlet molds* or in individual tart pans.

STEAMED PUDDINGS

Grease the pudding mold and put a round of greased wax paper in the base. Fill not more than two-thirds full with the pudding mixture to allow room for expansion during cooking. Cut a piece of double wax paper or foil to cover the mold and grease well. Make a pleat in the paper or foil in order to allow the pudding to rise.

Cover the mold tightly with the paper or foil and secure with string. If any moisture or water gets into the pudding it will sag or even collapse when turned out.

Place the mold in a large pan filled with boiling water to come halfway up the sides of the mold. Keep the water boiling rapidly all the time during steaming and have a kettle of boiling water on hand to top it up regularly. If you are using a saucepan and not a steamer the mold should be placed on a trivet—an upturned saucer or crossed skewers can be used—to keep the mold off the bottom of the pan. Keep the water gently bubbling so the mold just wobbles.
To turn out a steamed pudding:
Loosen the pudding at one side to let in some air, then invert it on to a warmed serving plate.

TO REHEAT A STEAMED PUDDING
Wrap the pudding in foil and heat through in a 350°F oven for 15–20 minutes.

TO COOK IN A PRESSURE COOKER
For a 1-quart pudding, pour about $3\frac{3}{4}$ cups water into the bottom of the pressure cooker. Stand the pudding on a trivet and steam without pressure for 15 minutes, then bring to low pressure and cook for about 2 hours depending on the pudding. Release pressure slowly.

IRRESISTIBLE DESSERTS

Cooking with Fruits and Nuts

Fruits can make desserts so varied and delicious. Each fruit offers its own distinctive flavor and texture that it is worth trying as many types as possible when they are in season to make simple fruit salads or creamy mousses and sorbets. Dried fruits and nuts extend the choice even further.

GLOSSARY OF FRESH FRUIT

APPLES
Apples are available all year round and are at their best in the autumn months. Cooking apples tend to be larger than eating apples. They are too tart to eat on their own but when cooked with sugar they have a wonderful sweet and sharp flavor. Cooking apples are juicy and will cook to a fluffy purée. When making purées add the sugar toward the end of cooking time. To help apples keep their shape add the sugar at the start of cooking. Look for Greenings, Northern Spies and Cortlands.

Eating apples often have more flavor than cooking apples. Macintosh, McCouns, Winesaps, Jonathans and Granny Smiths all have distinctive flavors, making them good additions to raw fruit salads and to pies, tarts and puddings. Less sugar is needed when cooking eating apples.

Avoid mealy tasteless apples. Look for firm apples with unblemished skins. Keep apples cool and dry. Apples kept at room temperature should be eaten within 2 weeks. Simply wipe and wash before eating.

To prepare them for cooking, apples are usually peeled and then quartered and cored. An apple corer is a handy gadget which makes coring easy and neat. Apple slices should be brushed with lemon juice to prevent browning.

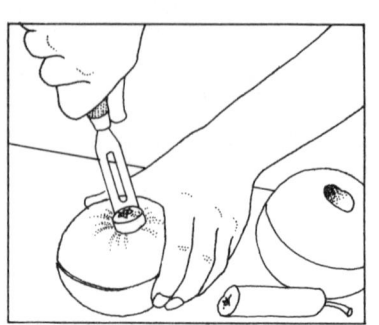

Removing cores with an apple corer

APRICOTS
Unripe apricots are hard and sour; overripe ones will be mealy and tasteless. Leave apricots to ripen at room temperature. Once ripe, they should be eaten within 2–3 days. Apricots are available for a relatively short period in spring and summer.

Cracking apricot kernels

Prepare apricots by washing, cutting them in half and removing the pit. To peel apricots, blanch in boiling water for 30 seconds to loosen the skins, then peel. Sliced apricots should be brushed with lemon juice to prevent browning. Apricot pits have a subtle almond flavor. Crack the kernels and use to flavor sugar syrups when poaching apricots.

BANANAS
Bananas for eating are picked hard and green. When buying look for evenly colored skins. They are ready to eat when yellow and slightly flecked brown. They will ripen if kept in the dark at room temperature. Once peeled, bananas should be brushed with lemon juice to prevent discoloring.

BLACKBERRIES
Blackberries ripen in late summer and early autumn. When buying, avoid stained containers as this may indicate crushed fruit below. Once picked, blackberries lose their flavor rapidly and if bought should be eaten on the same day.

COOKING WITH FRUITS AND NUTS

To prepare blackberries, wash them and remove the stalks. Remove any damaged fruit. Blackberries are especially good cooked with other fruit such as apples. They can be baked, bottled, eaten raw or frozen. Freeze only fully ripe undamaged fruit, without washing. Damaged or wet fruit can be cooked before freezing but will only keep for about 6 months.

BLUEBERRIES
Small berries that are very plentiful in summer. Choose firm ones. Wild blueberries are smaller and available only locally in Maine and other northern areas.

CHERRIES
Cherries are a summer fruit. A number of different types are available as the different varieties have a very short picking time. Avoid split, diseased or immature fruit. For raw eating cherries, look for large soft berries. Smaller tart varieties are better for cooking.

Prepare cherries by rinsing them in a colander and removing the stems. Cherry stoners are available for the purpose or you can cut into them with the point of a knife and pop out the stone.

Stringing currants with a fork

CURRANTS
Currants are ripe in midsummer and occasionally sold in markets. They are normally on a strip or stalk. Avoid withered or dusty currants; choose firm ones with a distinct gloss. To remove the currants from their stalks, use a fork to rake them off. Currants can be frozen raw, cooked or pulped. If storing in the refrigerator, keep covered for up to 10 days, removing damaged fruit.

GOOSEBERRIES
These are occasionally sold fresh. Unripe gooseberries are always green. As they ripen they turn gold, red or even white; some of them bear tails. Buy evenly colored fruit, keep it refrigerated and eat within 3 days. Wash the gooseberries and snip off the tail and flower ends; discard damaged fruit. Gooseberries are sour and will always need sweetening. For puddings, slightly immature fruits are better.

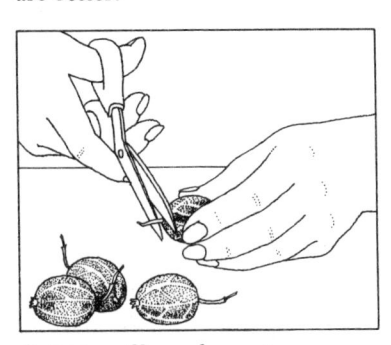

Snipping off gooseberry stems

Ripe gooseberries do not freeze well but barely or under ripe fruit can be frozen. Cooked gooseberries stewed or pulped will keep frozen for up to 1 year.

GRAPEFRUIT
These large citrus fruits are always available. Select evenly colored glossy fruit. They will keep for 4 days at room temperature and 2 weeks refrigerated.

Prepare grapefruit by cutting in half and separating the flesh from the skin with a serrated knife. Then divide the segments. Or, peel the skin off cutting just below the pith, then hold the fruit in one

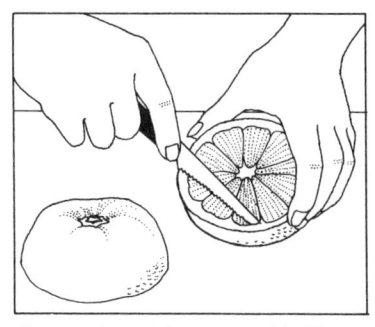

Segmenting with a serrated knife

hand and cut out the segments with the other leaving the protective membrane behind.

GRAPES
Grapes can range from pale amber to a deep blue color. Buy plump unbruised grapes still attached to their stems. Keep grapes refrigerated and use within 3 days. Grapes should be left unwashed until ready to serve. Seeds can be removed by halving the fruit with a knife and flicking out the seeds with a knife. To leave the fruit whole, push a sterilized pin into the grape and push out the seeds. Remove the skins by placing grapes in boiling water for 20 seconds; the skins can then be peeled off with a knife. Black grapes are not usually peeled.

KIWI FRUIT
(Chinese gooseberries)
Available from midsummer to late winter, kiwi fruit are egg shaped with a brown furry skin. Ripeness is tested by gentle pressure and a slight yielding of the flesh. Kiwi fruit should be kept at room temperature until ripe and then used within 2 days. Preparation simply consists of peeling the fruit with a small sharp knife and slicing the bright green flesh crossways. There is a pleasant pattern of edible black seeds in the flesh.

133

KUMQUATS

Kumquats are very small members of the orange family, about the size of a plum. They are available all the year round. They should have smooth shiny skins; avoid those with shriveled skins. They can be stored at room temperature for up to 2 days and refrigerated for up to 1 week. Prepare kumquats by rinsing them (in a colander) and removing the stems. Halve lengthways or leave whole, and slice thinly for dessert decoration. Both the skin and flesh are eaten and they are best when poached.

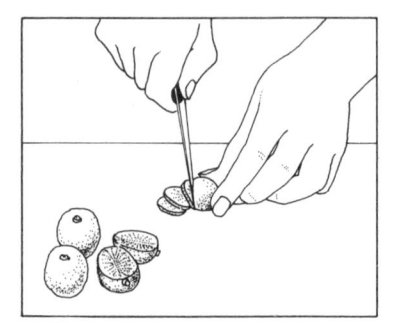

Slicing kumquats thinly

LEMONS AND LIMES

Lemons and limes are available all year round, though limes are not sold as widely as lemons. Limes are greener than lemons (the darker the color the better) and slightly smaller but for preparation limes may be treated the same way as lemons. Look for lemons which are a strong lemon-yellow color and have a moist-looking skin; they should feel heavy for their size. A shriveled skin will indicate that some of the juice has evaporated. Lemons will be at their best for only a few days if kept at room temperature and up to 2 weeks in the refrigerator.

To extract the maximum amount of juice from a lemon or lime, it should be at room temperature. Roll the fruit back and forth in your hands, pressing gently with the palm to help soften the fruit. Then slice the fruit in half crosswise and either squeeze hard or use a lemon squeezer. *One large lemon contains about 2 Tbsp juice.*

The skins of limes are tougher and much thinner than those of lemons and so release much less zest. When grating lemon zest make sure that none of the bitter tasting white pith is grated. To thinly pare lemons, peel the rind with a vegetable peeler, again avoiding any of the bitter white pith.

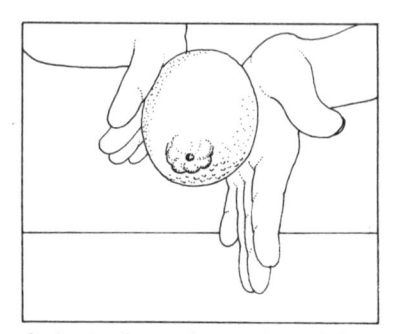

Softening lemon for maximum juice

MANGOES

Mangoes are available most of the year except in early winter. Ripe mangoes are very juicy and have a yellow or orange skin; they should give to a gentle squeeze. Avoid soft or shriveled mangoes. Ripe mangoes should be kept and used within 3 days.

To prepare mangoes, cut a large slice from one side of the fruit, cutting close to the pit. Cut another slice from the opposite side. The flesh in the cut segments can be scooped out into squares lengthwise and crosswise without breaking the skin. Push the skin inside out to expose the cubes of flesh. Use a sharp knife to peel the remaining center section and cut the flesh away from the pit in chunks or slices.

MELONS

Melons are available all year round except for watermelons, which are only available in summer, the time of year when melons are most abundantly available. Depending on the variety, melons can be smooth skinned or have a light or heavy netting. Many have a light or heavy ridging—conveniently the ridges can be used as guides for serving portions. All melons have a highly perfumed sweet juicy flesh. Usually, the more fragrant the melon the sweeter and juicier its flesh will be.

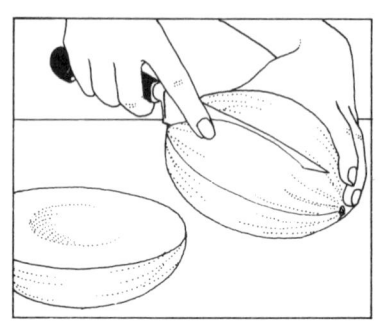

Cutting melon into wedges

Melons should be stored tightly wrapped in the refrigerator as they can easily pick up the flavor of other foods. Ripe melons are firm but have a slight give when pressed at the ends. Use within 2–3 days. Soft patches on the rind indicate bruising rather than ripeness. Buy slices or wedges only if they have been kept with the cut surface covered with plastic wrap.

TO SERVE ROUND MELONS

Cut melons in half crosswise and scoop out the seeds with a spoon. They will look more attractive if the edges are cut in a zig-zag pattern. To use the halves as *melon bowls*, cut a small slice off the bottom of each half so they stand upright. Keep the bowls tightly wrapped in the refrigerator until ready to serve.

COOKING WITH FRUITS AND NUTS

TO MAKE MELON WEDGES
Halve fruit lengthwise, scoop out seeds and cut into wedges. Cut the flesh free from the rind, but leave in place; divide it into cubes.

TO MAKE MELON BALLS
Scoop out the melon flesh with a melon baller.

NECTARINES
Nectarines can be bought from midsummer to early autumn and from early winter into the spring. Shop for plump rich-colored fruit softening along the indent. Hard, extremely soft or shriveled fruit should be avoided. Nectarines will ripen at room temperature but once ripened should be refrigerated and used within a period of 5 days.

Preparation is simply washing. They may be peeled with a sharp knife if desired then halved and pitted. Brush the exposed flesh with lemon juice to stop discoloring.

ORANGES
Oranges are at their best in the early months of the year. Choose firm fruit that feel heavy and have a glossy skin. Avoid those with dry or hard looking skins. Thick-skinned navel oranges are easy to peel and are seedless; thinner-skinned oranges are more difficult to peel but are usually more juicy and have a more pronounced orange flavor.

Oranges will keep for 4 days at room temperature and if wrapped

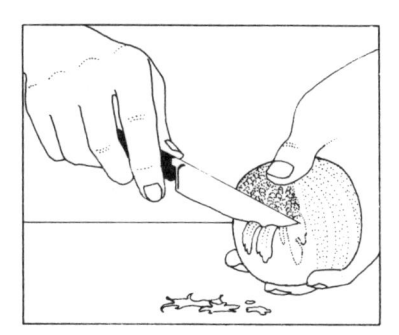

Scraping off the white pith

and stored in the refrigerator they will keep for at least 2 weeks.

When serving sliced oranges the white pith should be scraped off with a knife after the orange is peeled. When dividing the oranges into segments hold the fruit over a bowl to catch all the juices. The pith is more easily removed from warm oranges than cold ones. Pour over boiling water to cover and leave the oranges for several minutes before peeling.

To use orange peel in cooking, peel the rind with a vegetable peeler avoiding any of the bitter white pith, then blanch the peel for 3 minutes, rinse under cold water and then shred before using.

PEACHES
Peaches are at their best in early summer. Ripe peaches are slightly soft and have a yellow to orange skin. Avoid green, bruised or "sale" fruit. Eat peaches within 2 days if kept at room temperature or if wrapped and chilled within 5 days. Peaches can be peeled by immersing them in boiling water for about 15 seconds, then cooking in cold water. Use a sharp knife to separate the loosened skin from the flesh. Very ripe peaches are best if skinned and pitted under running water, as scalding them will soften and slightly discolor the flesh. Cut lengthways along the indentation in the fruit and twist the fruit in half, then remove the stone. Brush cut fruit with lemon juice to prevent browning.

PEARS
Pears are available all the year round. Buy well-formed firm pears with no oozing or softness. Ripe pears give a little at the stem end. They do not remain ripe for long and so should be checked often. They will ripen indoors but then should be refrigerated and used within 3 days. For eating raw, Williams, Comice or Anjou's are good. Use firm pears for cooking.

TO MAKE A MELON BASKET
Honeydews and watermelons can be used to make large baskets and small round melons such as cantaloupe can be used to make individual baskets. Cut a thin slice off the bottom of the melon so it will stand upright. Make 2 cuts each about ½ inch from the top stem of the melon and cut straight down to the center of the melon. Then slice horizontally to make 2 wedges; remove the wedges. Remove the seeds from the center of the melon and evenly cut away the flesh from the piece that is forming the basket handle. Scoop out the melon flesh discarding seeds if using a watermelon. Chill, tightly wrapped, until required.

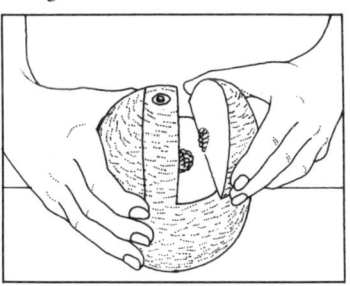

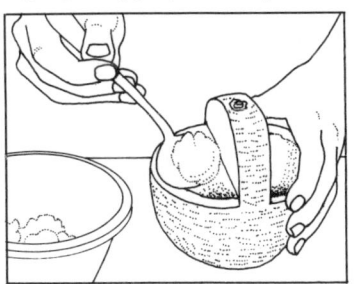

Removing wedges to make handle

Scooping out flesh with a spoon

IRRESISTIBLE DESSERTS

Prepare pears by washing and peeling; scoop out the core with a teaspoon. A pear wedger will core

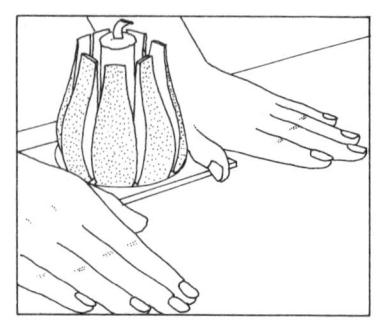

Slicing and coring with a wedger

and cut a pear quickly. Lemon juice will prevent slow deterioration of peeled pears.

PINEAPPLES
Pineapples are available all year round. Ripe pineapples give off a sweet aroma and in addition a leaf will pull easily from the crown. Avoid pineapples that are bruised or discolored or have wilting leaves. These fruits continue to ripen after picking and are often sold slightly unripe. However a really unripe pineapple with no aroma will not ripen properly. The most common method of preparation is to cut off the leaf crown and cut the pineapple into thick slices crossways. Use the tip of the blade to trim off the outer skin and remove the tiny brown spots from the flesh. Use either a small knife or an apple corer to remove the central core. Pineapples can also be served in wedges. Cut the fruit in half and

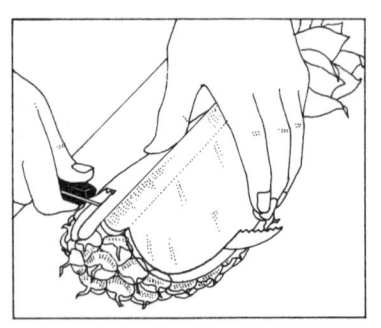

Separating pineapple flesh

then quarters lengthways, cutting through but not removing the leaf crown. Use a small knife to cut out the exposed central core. Use a curved knife to separate the flesh from the skin and cut it downwards in order to make wedge-shaped slices.

PLUMS
The different varieties of this fruit are available from the late spring to early autumn. The color may vary from yellow or green to red or almost black. Hard, shriveled or split plums should be avoided. Sweet plums can be eaten raw and all varieties can be cooked. Sweet or dessert plums will ripen at home in a few days. Greengages are sweet, light green-colored plums; deep purple damsons are good all-rounders.

Prepare plums by washing and halving them. Pits can be removed with the tip of a knife.

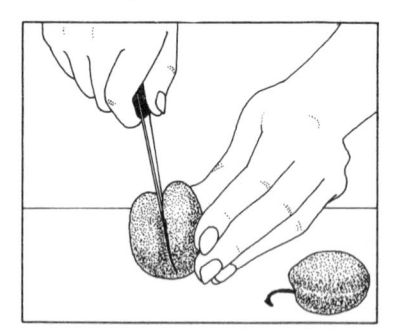

Halving damsons with a knife

Plums freeze well, preferably top-quality just ripe fruit. The pits if left in during the cooking will produce an almond-like flavor. Some varieties of plum skin hardens in freezing. If freezing in sugar syrup add ascorbic acid or lemon juice.

POMEGRANATES
Pomegranates are available in the autumn. Buy fruit with hard russet-colored skin. Keep pomegranates refrigerated and use within 7 days. Prepare by cutting a slice off the stem end with a sharp knife. Then slice the skin sections lengthways and draw the sections

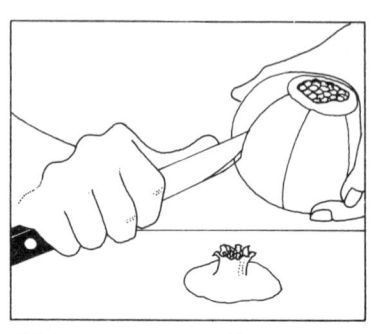

Slicing pomegranate skin

apart. Push in the skin and push out the seeds from the inside. Seeds can be eaten or juiced. Pomegranates should not be frozen.

QUINCES
Quinces are available in October to November. Avoid scabby, split or small fruit. The apple-shaped quinces stew well and the pear-shaped ones keep well. Store them in a cool dry place away from absorbent foods likely to be affected by the strong aroma of quinces. A few quinces are eaten raw but most are cooked with other fruit, especially apples. To prepare quinces simply peel and slice or chop.

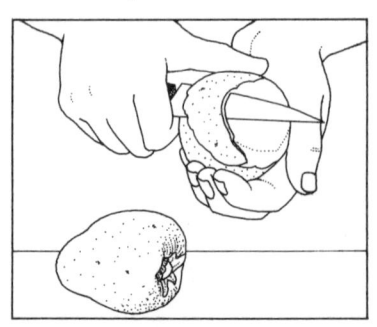

Peeling quinces with a sharp knife

RASPBERRIES
The main season for raspberries is from late June to mid August although some varieties are sold into early autumn. Raspberries are sold hulled which makes them liable to crushing. When shopping avoid stained containers and wet fruit

COOKING WITH FRUITS AND NUTS

especially. After damp weather they are likely to mold quickly; any deteriorating fruit should be discarded as soon as possible. Use only the best dry fruit at the point of ripening when freezing. Over-ripe or damaged fruit may be sieved and frozen as pulp.

RHUBARB
Rhubarb comes in spring and early summer. It has a strong color and a thick stem and is sharp in taste. Rhubarb should be kept cool or refrigerated and used within 4 days. If rhubarb looks a little limp it can be stood, leaf up, in cold water, like flowers, to crispen. To prepare rhubarb, chop off and discard the leaves and root ends and wash the stems. Some rhubarbs have a tougher stem which may need peeling. Chop the

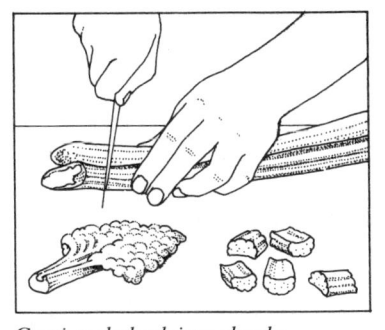

Cutting rhubarb into chunks

stems into chunks for cooking. For short-term freezing trim the ends, wash, drain and freeze. For longer freezing blanch it in boiling water for 1 minute.

CLEMENTINES AND TANGERINES
Look for these fruits in the winter months. Choose small loose-skinned varieties with a bright orange color. Avoid dry ones or those with patches of soft skin. They will keep at room temperature for a few days or if kept

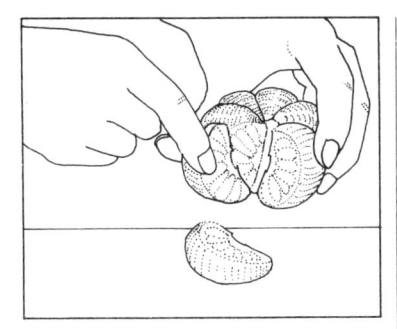

Segmenting a clementine/tangerine

refrigerated up to 10 days. The skin does not cling to the flesh and can be peeled off by hand. Pick off remaining bits of white pith. Divide the fruit into segments, eat raw or in salads.

STRAWBERRIES
A true summer fruit, the majority available in July. As with most berries check the base of the container for staining as this will indicate squashed fruit. Strawberries are probably most famous for being eaten raw, with cream but are also delicious puréed and chilled. Be sure to buy plump glossy berries with their green frills still attached. Only wash berries just before hulling. Sugared, hulled strawberries yield the juice readily. Besides eating, raw strawberries can be stewed and put into flans, tarts and pies. Freeze only the best just ripe fruit. Damaged or over-ripe fruit can be frozen as pulp with a little lemon juice or citric acid added.

Puréeing strawberries with a sieve

UNUSUAL FRUITS
The variety of fruits available seems to be ever increasing as we see more and more unusual looking fruits in markets bearing prickly wrinkled skins, odd shapes and often giving off exotically perfumed aromas. These fruits are often very expensive but can be bought in very small quantities and used to liven up fruit salads or to make unusual decorations for puddings. In a moment of extravagance they can be used to make very special sorbets. Many of them are available canned. Preparing them need not be a mystery.

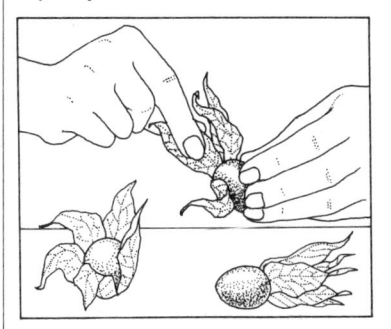

Bending calyx on cape gooseberries

Cape gooseberry or Chinese lantern. When ripe, the berries are enclosed in a lantern-shaped case or calyx, and are orange yellow in color. If the case or calyx is bent back to form a petal around the central berry, they can be used as a decoration for cakes. They can also be eaten raw or added to fruit salads.

137

IRRESISTIBLE DESSERTS

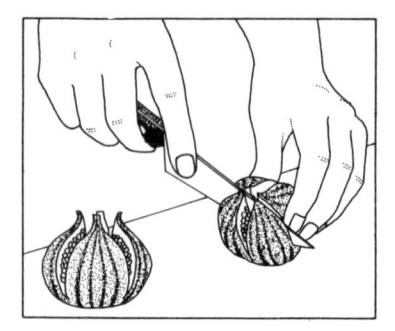

Slicing and opening figs for serving

Figs. These can be simply sliced or partially sliced and opened like a flower. They are juicy and have a more delicate flavor than their more frequently used dried counterpart.

Guavas. A juicy fruit full of seeds, guavas can be pear-shaped, or round looking like tomatoes. They should be peeled then puréed or baked.

Breaking and peeling lychee skin

Lychees. The hard, red-brown scaly skin should be broken and then peeled. The white pulpy flesh surrounds a soft brown stone. Remove the stone and serve the lychees chilled. They have a distinctive flavor—slightly acid yet sweet.

Papaya. A large smooth-skinned fruit which ripens from green to yellow to orange. Slice the fruit in half and remove the black seeds in the center. Cut into slices and add to fruit salads—papayas have a smooth soft texture and a distinctive rich flavor.

Passion fruit. Most varieties we see have a hard brown wrinkled skin. Slice the fruit in half and scoop out the flesh with a teaspoon; the seeds can be eaten and when passion fruit is used in fruit creams and sorbets the seeds should be included in the purée.

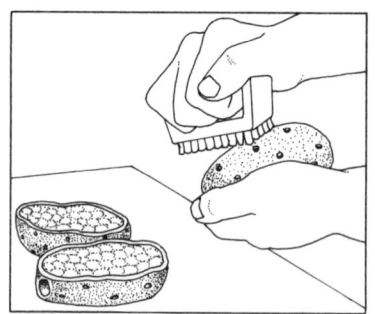

Scrubbing prickles off prickly pear

Prickly pear. A prickly pear has a greenish-orange skin covered with tiny prickles. The sweet juicy pink flesh has edible seeds. Wash and scrub off the prickles, cut off each end, slit downwards and peel back the skin. Slice the flesh and serve with a squeeze of lemon juice.

Halving persimmon with a knife

Persimmon. The most frequently found variety of persimmon is the oriental persimmon. It looks like a large plump tomato and has a sweet, slightly sour tasting flesh. It is seedless and both skin and flesh are eaten. The flesh can be puréed and used in many types of ice creams and mousses.

FRUIT SAUCES

The distinctive flavors of fruit sauces will add enormously to the enjoyment of your desserts. Because fruit sauces are often sharp and tangy as well as quite sweet, they can be the perfect complement to bland desserts such as meringues, cold soufflés, crêpes or simple puddings. They come into their own when poured over vanilla ice cream.

Fruit sauces are very simple to make. Usually a purée of fruit is sweetened and lightly thickened. *Cornstarch* is always first dissolved in a cold liquid before it is added to a hot one, otherwise it will be lumpy. Cornstarch-thickened sauces need to be cooked to remove the raw taste of the starch; during this time the sauce thickens. A sauce thickened with *arrowroot* will be clear and shiny but it should be served soon after making as arrowroot soon loses its thickening properties.

FRUIT SAUCE

Makes 1¼ cups

15-oz can fruit in syrup
2 tsp arrowroot or cornstarch
squeeze of lemon juice (optional)

1 Strain the juice from the fruit. Sieve the fruit, make up to 1¼ cups with juice and heat until boiling.

2 Blend the arrowroot with a little of the unused fruit juice until it is a smooth cream and stir in the puréed fruit. Return the mixture to the pan and heat gently, continuing to stir, until the sauce thickens and clears. Stir in the lemon juice if using.

——— VARIATION ———

Omit the lemon juice. Add 1 Tbsp rum, sherry or fruit liqueur to the sauce immediately before serving.

BLUEBERRY SAUCE

Makes 2½ cups

1 lb blueberries, washed
1 cup water
1 Tbsp cornstarch
¾ cup sugar
pinch of salt
1 tsp lemon juice

1 Trim the berries. Bring the water to the boil, add the berries and bring back to the boil.

2 Meanwhile, mix the cornstarch to a smooth paste with a little cold water. Stir it into the berries with the sugar and salt and cook until the mixture has thickened, stirring constantly, then add the lemon juice.

STRAWBERRY SAUCE

Makes 2 cups

1 pint strawberries, washed
¼ cup sugar
1¼ cups water
juice of 1 orange
1 Tbsp cornstarch

1 Trim the berries. Put the sugar and water into a large saucepan and heat gently until the sugar has completely dissolved. Add the berries and simmer until they are tender.

2 Mix the orange juice with the cornstarch, stir in a little of the strawberry juice and pour the mixture into the sauce, stirring well. Bring to the boil and simmer for 1–2 minutes until the sauce has thickened.

CREAMY PLUM SAUCE

Makes 2 cups

4 eating plums, washed
2 cups confectioners sugar
8 oz cream cheese, softened

1 Halve and pit the plums. Put them in a blender with the sugar and blend until smooth, or rub through sieve to remove skins.

2 Add the cream cheese and beat until well blended. Cover and chill until required.

BRANDIED CHERRY SAUCE

Makes 2 cups

1 lb cherries, washed and pitted
½ cup brandy
½ cup sugar
2 tsp cornstarch
1 tsp almond extract

Put the cherries into a large saucepan with the brandy, sugar and cornstarch and cook, stirring all the time, until the mixture has thickened and just begins to boil. Remove from the heat and stir in the almond extract.

MELBA SAUCE

Makes 2 cups

1 lb raspberries
4 Tbsp red currant jelly
1 Tbsp confectioners sugar
2 Tbsp arrowroot
1 Tbsp water

1 Rub the raspberries through a sieve into a saucepan. Add the jelly and sugar and bring to boil.

2 Blend the arrowroot with the cold water to a smooth cream and stir in a little of the raspberry mixture. Return the sauce to the pan and bring to the boil, stirring with a wooden spoon, until it thickens and clears. Strain and leave to cool.

FRUIT PURÉES

Many fruit sauces are based on purées. Usually the fruit is first cooked with sugar until softened. Soft berry fruits however are sometimes not cooked before puréeing. The softened fruit is rubbed through a sieve which should be nylon, as metal can sometimes react with the acid in the fruit and taint the flavor. Although it is much simpler to purée the fruit in a blender or food processor it may still be necessary to sieve the fruit in order to remove any small seeds. A fruit purée can make a simple dessert on its own served with cream.

FRUIT GLAZES

Glazes not only give fruit flans and tarts a shiny covering but they also help protect the fruits from discoloring or drying out.

When making fruit glazes use a jam which complements the color of the fruit to be covered. About ⅔ cup glaze is enough to cover two 8-inch tarts.

APRICOT GLAZE

Makes ⅔ cup

4 oz apricot jam
2 Tbsp water

Glazing a fruit tart

Sieve the jam into a small saucepan and add the water. Heat gently, stirring, until the jam softens. Bring to the boil and simmer for 1 minute. Allow to cool until warm then spoon over the flan or tart.

———— VARIATION ————

Red currant Use red currant jelly instead of apricot jam; there is no need to sieve the jelly, just stir until completely blended.

DRIED FRUITS

Dried fruits add a concentrated natural sweetness to a number of desserts. Keep them in the cupboard as a useful standby for making winter fruit salads and fruit compotes.

Although dried fruit is most frequently bought in small packages, large packages of raisins are a more economical buy as are dried fruits sold loose or in bulk from some health food shops. Packaged dried fruits are always pre-washed but fruit sold loose should be washed.

Store dried fruit in a cool, dark place. Unopened packages will keep for up to 1 year. Once opened or if bought loose, store the fruit in an airtight tin. For best flavor use within 3 months.

To make interesting fruit salads select from the more unusual variety of dried fruits like *pears*, *peaches*, *apples* and *bananas*. Dried bananas look like elongated figs and should not be confused with the sweetened banana chips which are usually eaten as a snack food. Dried *apricots* have a more pronounced and usually better flavor than their fresh counterpart and when reconstituted can be used to make flans, tarts and pies in the same way as fresh apricots.

For making attractive cake decorations choose from the large variety of candied fruits. These fruits which are preserved in sugar syrup can have a glossy coating, in which case they are known as *glacé fruits*, or they will have a granulated coating, when they are known as *crystallized fruits*. Candied fruits are widely available at Christmas time when they are served in fruit cakes and mince pies. Leftovers can be chopped and used to decorate puddings.

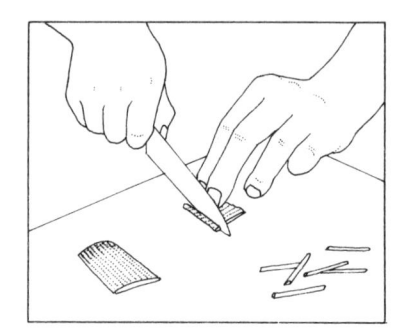

Cutting angelica into strips

TO MAKE ANGELICA LEAVES
Cut the angelica into $\frac{1}{4}$-inch strips, then cut each strip into diagonal slices.

Angelica is a traditional decoration. Look for angelica with a good green color. Large pieces of *candied peel* are preferable to the ready-chopped peel. Freshly cut candied peel will have more aroma and flavor. Peel can be cut into slivers and used to decorate cold soufflés and mousses, in an attractive border. *Crystallized violets and roses* can also be used for decorating. Buy them in small quantities and store them in a cool, dark place to avoid bleaching. *Glacé cherries* are used whole or sliced for decorating; they come in red, green and gold colors.

Store all candied fruits in a cool, dry place and use within 6 months.

TO CLEAN DRIED FRUIT
Wash the fruit, removing any stalks or leaves, and spread them out over cheesecloth or absorbent paper towels on a wire rack. Leave them to dry for 2–3 hours. Alternatively, to quickly clean the fruit, rub the fruit on a wire sieve or in a tea towel with a little flour, then pick over to remove any stalk. Do not dry fruit over direct heat as this tends to make them hard.

TO PLUMP DRIED FRUIT
Prunes and raisins can become hard during storage and currants are naturally hard. These fruits can be plumped in a little hot water or some of the recipe liquid for about 30 minutes before using. Soaking them in sherry or brandy will add extra flavor.

TO SOAK DRIED FRUIT
Other dried fruits should be soaked for at least 3 hours or even overnight. Soak the fruit in cold water, but to shorten the soaking time pour boiling water over to cover and leave the fruits to soak. Prunes will taste better if soaked in cold tea or red wine. Dried fruit doubles its weight when soaked. No-need-to-soak apricots and prunes are available and these require no preparation.

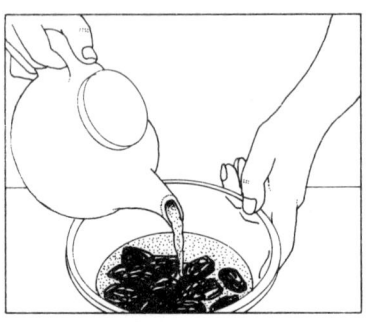

Soaking prunes in cold tea

TO CHOP DRIED FRUIT
Dried fruit can be chopped in the same way as nuts. They can also be snipped with scissors. To prevent the fruits from sticking, lightly flour them or use confectioners sugar. Sugar-dusted chopped dates are available.

TO STEW DRIED FRUIT
Cook them in the soaking water adding ½ cup sugar and a small piece of lemon rind to every 2½ cups water. Stew gently until soft and serve hot or cold with custard sauce.

TO REMOVE THE SUGARY COATING FROM GLACÉ FRUITS
The glossy coating on cherries and other glacéed fruits should be removed before they are used in baking; otherwise the fruit will sink to the bottom of the pan as it is dragged down by the sugary coating. Rinse the fruit under warm running water and pat dry with paper towels.

Tossing glacé cherries in flour

Toss the fruit in a little of the recipe flour before adding to the pudding or cake mixture. Glacé fruits used to decorate desserts will lose their luster if washed, but the sugary coating also tends to seep on the topping if they are applied much in advance of serving.

NUTS

The more that nuts have been prepared by the producer the more convenient they will be to use, but they will usually be more expensive than the whole nuts. Nuts prepared at home will also have more flavor because they will have had less chance to dry out and lose their aromatic properties. Ready-shelled nuts are much more convenient to have on hand than whole nuts. Do not use flavored or salted nuts in desserts.

Buying nuts in bulk can be economical but the high fat content in nuts means that they can become rancid, especially walnuts, pecans and peanuts. Ideally nuts should be used within 1 month and kept stored in a cool place in an airtight tin. To extend their shelf life, nuts can be very successfully frozen and usually can be used from frozen without thawing. Old nuts can be crisped in the oven before using.

Of all the nuts used in dessert making, none is more versatile than *almonds* with their sweet distinctive flavor. They are sold whole in their skins, blanched, slivered, sliced, and ground. Almonds are widely used to make decorations on cakes and cookies. *Praline* is a combination of sugar and almonds which is crushed to make a dessert topping or it can be folded into ice cream mixtures and meringues. *Hazelnuts* are another popular dessert-making nut. Besides being used finely chopped for dessert toppings, they are also folded into meringues and ice creams. Hazelnuts can also be used to make praline. Whole, chopped and ground hazelnuts are available. *Brazilnuts* are usually eaten as a sweetmeat, sometimes dipped in chocolate, but the large nut can also be flaked by using a vegetable peeler and then toasted and used as a decoration. Finely chopped *walnuts* added to crumb crusts gives them a fuller, richer flavor and walnuts are a welcome addition to hot sauces for ice creams and puddings. Walnuts can be successfully substituted for the more expensive *pecans*, a nut with a very soft texture and rich mild flavor. *Cashews, peanuts, pistachio nuts* and *macadamia nuts* all can be used to add interesting variations to puddings and dessert decorations; use coarsely chopped and sprinkled over cold desserts.

TO BLANCH ALMONDS
Nuts are blanched by being boiled briefly and then skinned. Place almonds in a pan of cold water, bring just to the boil, then strain and run under cold water. The skin can be easily slipped off be-

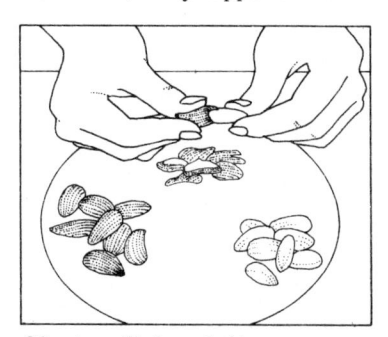

Slipping off almond skins

tween the thumb and finger. Freshly blanched almonds are more easily chopped or flaked.

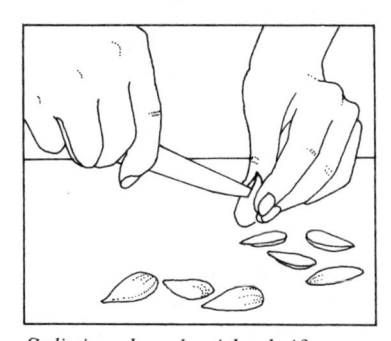

Splitting almonds with a knife

TO SPLIT ALMONDS
Almonds can be split by inserting the tip of a very sharp knife between the two halves of the nut and separating them.

TO SKIN HAZELNUTS AND PEANUTS

The thin inner covering of shelled nuts is usually peeled because it has a bitter taste. Heat the nuts in the oven or toast under a low broiler. Tip the hot nuts into a clean cloth and rub until the papery skins slip off.

TO TOAST AND ROAST NUTS

The flavor of nuts is often more pronounced if they are first toasted. Pale-colored almonds turn a golden color, making them especially attractive for dessert decorations. Spread whole, chopped or slivered nuts on a baking tray and toast them under a medium broiler, turning the nuts occasionally, until they have darkened. Alternatively, they can be roasted in a 350°F oven for 10–12 minutes. Nuts can also be dry fried in a frying pan for about 5 minutes. Watch nuts carefully as they can suddenly burn.

TO CHOP NUTS

Nuts can be simply chopped on a board using a long, sharp knife.

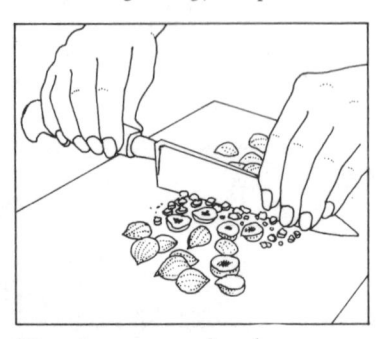

Chopping nuts on a board

Gather the nuts into a pile against the flat of a knife and slice firmly through the nuts, with the knife held against your finger. Steady the tip of the blade with your hand and chop rapidly. Keep collecting the nuts into a pile and repeat chopping until chopped to the desired size.

Because of the shape and hard texture of hazelnuts they are more easily chopped in a very clean coffee grinder. A food processor can also be used for chopping nuts but care must be taken when using these machines that the nuts do not grind to a flour or paste.

TO GRIND NUTS

Nuts ground at home will have more flavor and aroma than bought ones. Almonds and hazelnuts are often used ground, especially almonds for making marzipan. Ground nuts are good to sprinkle over a tart shell before filling with a juicy fruit filling—they help to absorb the fruit juices and ensure the baked blind crust remains crisp as well as adding extra flavor.

Grind nuts in a coffee grinder or food processor. Grind for about 1 minute turning the grinder on and off frequently during grinding. Only grind a little at a time. Be careful that the nuts do not turn to a paste.

PRALINE

Makes about $\frac{3}{4}$ cup

$\frac{1}{2}$ cup granulated sugar
$\frac{1}{4}$ cup blanched almonds, chopped and toasted

1 Oil a baking sheet. Place the sugar with 4 Tbsp water in a saucepan and heat gently, stirring all the time, until the sugar dissolves. Bring to the boil and boil steadily, without stirring, until golden brown.

2 Add the almonds and pour at once on to the prepared baking sheet. Leave to set for about 10 minutes.

3 Crush the praline finely with a rolling pin or in a food processor or blender.

COCONUTS

To prepare a coconut, puncture the shell at the eyes with a screwdriver and hammer. Drain the water into a bowl. Store, covered, in the refrigerator for up to 2 days. (Use to make drinks.) Crack the shell by hitting the widest part of the coconut all around with a hammer or the back of a cleaver.

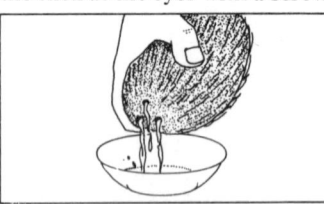

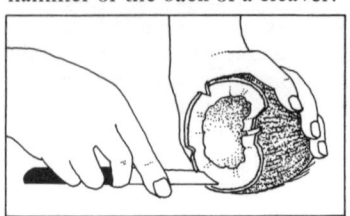

Separate the halves and pry the flesh from the shell with a small sharp knife.

TO SHRED AND TOAST COCONUT

Using a sharp knife remove the rough brown skin and shred the white flesh on a coarse grater or grate in a food processor or blender. Freshly grated coconut can be toasted in a 350°F oven until golden brown.

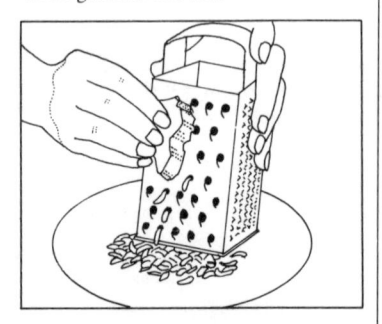

Stir the coconut frequently. Store up to 4 days.

Shredded coconut is available in stores mostly sweetened but also occasionally unsweetened.

Cooking with Chocolate and Cream

Chocolate and cream are probably the most popular and versatile of dessert ingredients—whether used as part of the dessert itself or as an attractive and mouth-watering finishing touch. Use them separately or, for extra richness, together.

CHOCOLATE

Cocoa powder is often used in cakes and puddings. As it is unsweetened, sugar must be added in order for it to be palatable.

Unsweetened chocolate is used exclusively in cooking, since it contains no sugar. It is not used as a garnish.

Semisweet chocolate has a small amount of sugar and may be labelled *bitter* or *semisweet* depending on its sugar content.

TO MELT CHOCOLATE

Chocolate can suddenly burn and so needs to be very gently melted. Break into small pieces and place them in the top of a double boiler over hot, but not boiling, water. Leave until melted. Be sure to keep both water and steam away from the melting chocolate, as the chocolate can become grainy and lose its smooth appearance if moisture gets into it.

Chocolate can also be melted in a 225°F oven. Place the pieces in an ovenproof bowl and leave until melted. If you melt the chocolate over direct heat, use a heavy-based saucepan and stir constantly with a wooden spoon to prevent the chocolate burning. When adding chocolate to hot liquids like custards and milk, remove the hot liquid from the heat and stir in pieces of chocolate to evenly blend.

If melted chocolate thickens or curdles because it has become too hot add a little solid vegetable shortening. Break into small pieces and stir into mixture until it reaches desired consistency.

DECORATING WITH CHOCOLATE

Chocolate decorations make desserts look more appetizing, and they add a little extra flavor. Use chocolate to decorate coffee, orange, strawberry, mint and vanilla-flavored puddings. There are a number of ways to decorate with chocolate. Whichever way it is used, handle the chocolate as little as possible. Body heat melts chocolate and leaves fingerprints on the surface. Use a hard semisweet chocolate for chopping and grating; a soft chocolate like milk chocolate can be used to make curls and shapes.

Simplest chocolate decorations can consist of chocolate *sugar strands* (vermicelli) or crumbled *chocolate flake* sprinkled over a pudding. Semisweet chocolate can be grated by peeling off flakes or

Grating with a vegetable peeler

curls from the edge of a bar of chocolate with a swivel-bladed vegetable peeler. It is wise to keep the chocolate being grated in its wrapper except for the surface being grated to help prevent the chocolate melting.

For more interesting decorations pour melted chocolate on to a cool marble slab or baking tray, making a thin layer. Leave it to cool until it loses its tackiness and make either of the following:

IRRESISTIBLE DESSERTS

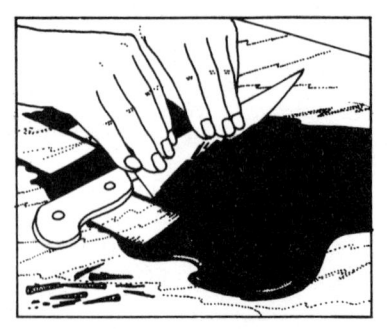

Making chocolate caraque

Caraque Use a long sharp knife and hold the blade in both hands. Push or draw the knife sideways across the surface of the chocolate making curls. By adjusting the angle at which the knife is held you will vary the size of the curls.

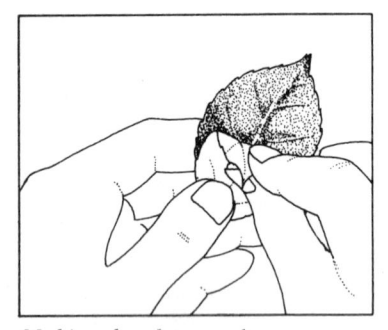

Making chocolate rose leaves

Leaves Using a knife, thinly spread melted chocolate on the undersides of clean, dry, un-damaged rose leaves. Leave to set. Gently peel leaf off chocolate.

Stamping out chocolate shapes

Shapes Cut the chocolate into neat triangles or squares with a sharp knife or use petits fours cutters to stamp out other shapes.

CREAM

Whipping cream will whip to at least double its volume. When vanilla flavoring and sugar are added to whipping cream, it becomes chantilly cream.

Light cream or half and half are used in some desserts. These are ideal pouring creams; they will not whip.

Sour cream has a slightly sour taste and is thick and spoonable. It will not whip, but is excellent for serving with puddings or as an ingredient in cakes for a tangy flavor.

Yogurt is similar to sour cream, but it is made from milk instead of cream. It is a delicious alternative to sour cream or whipping cream.

ICE CREAMS AND SORBETS

The knack of successfully making creamy smooth ice creams and sorbets largely involves making sure that no large ice crystals form during freezing. When making ice creams and sorbets without special

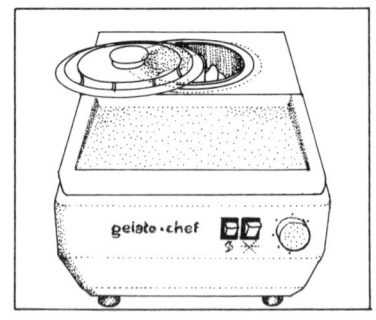

An electric ice cream maker

equipment it is necessary to periodically whisk the freezing mixture until smooth. Electric ice cream makers make superior ice cream without ice crystals.

When making ice cream and sorbets without a machine, the freezer should be turned to fast freeze or to its lowest setting because the quicker the mixture freezes the less likely the risk of crystallization. Sorbets are usually made with a sweetened fruit purée or juice. It must be highly flavored and sweetened as freezing diminishes sweetness and flavor. Too much sugar and the mixture will not freeze properly; too little sugar and the mixture turns to a block of ice. Some sorbets are made with the addition of egg whites which are folded into the mixture once it has partially frozen. This helps prevent large ice crystals forming.

Transfer ice creams and sorbets from the freezer to the refrigerator at least 30 minutes before serving to soften. Ice cream can be stored in the freezer for up to 3 months. Sorbets are best eaten within 1 month of making as they gradually develop ice crystals.

Cooking with Eggs

Eggs are invaluable for making desserts. They make soufflés and mousses light and produce the creamy smooth texture of custards, sauces, and ice creams. But eggs are temperamental and special care is needed when using them to ensure success every time. Eggs have an added bonus — they are a hidden nutrient in seemingly indulgent desserts.

Egg whites become foamy by trapping air when whisked; this special property enables them to act as a raising agent for batters and cakes, either alone or in combination with the yolk. When whisked separately egg whites give soufflés and meringues their characteristic lightness. The coagulating or thickening property of egg yolks is what makes thick custards and sauces when heat is applied.

Eggs need to be cooked gently and slowly, otherwise they will become too tough.

Be sure to cook with the freshest eggs possible. A fresh egg broken on to a flat surface will have an upstanding yolk and the whites adhering to it. Old eggs will have thin runny whites. To test for freshness put the egg into a tumbler of cold water. If the egg is fresh it will lie flat at the bottom

Testing an egg for freshness

of the glass. If the egg tilts slightly it is starting to become old and if it floats it is very likely to be bad.

TO SEPARATE AN EGG
Give the egg a sharp knock against the side of a bowl or cup and

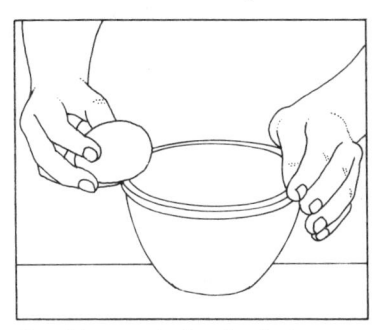

Breaking egg shell on bowl edge

break the shell in half; tapping the egg several times may cause it to crack in several places and not break evenly. Pass the yolk back and forth from one-half of the shell to the other letting the white drop into the bowl.

When separating more than one egg it is a good idea to use a third bowl for cracking the eggs as a precaution against a yolk breaking and spoiling the whites. Put the second yolk in with the first one and tip the white in with the first white. Continue using the third bowl in this way.

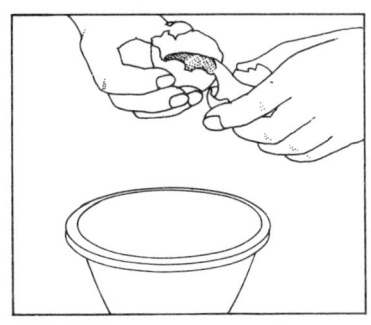

Separating egg yolk from white

EGG WHITES
When egg whites are whisked tiny globules of air are trapped in the egg to form an almost tasteless substance, which when added to other ingredients gives them an airy and light texture. If heat is applied to the egg whites the trapped air expands further

causing the mixture to rise further as in soufflés. Whisked egg whites also can become firm and hard without losing their shape, as in meringues.

Egg whites will achieve maximum volume when whisked in a metal bowl; copper is best but stainless steel is also good. Use a balloon whisk as a rotary or electric beater cannot be circulated as well throughout the eggs.

Eggs that are 2-3 days old will whisk to a greater volume than new laid eggs. For best results separate the eggs 24 hours before using them and store them in a covered container in the refrigerator. An acid such as cream of tartar added to the eggs or rubbing the bowl with lemon helps whites hold their shape when whisked.

What is important is that the bowl and the whisk or beaters are immaculately clean. If egg whites come into contact with any grease or dirt they will not whisk to maximum volume. Any egg yolk present in the whites will also decrease the volume. Salt also adversely affects the foaming of egg whites.

Start whisking with a slow circular movement and gradually work faster, lifting the eggs high out of the bowl to help incorporate as much air as possible. Whisk until the egg whites stand in stiff,

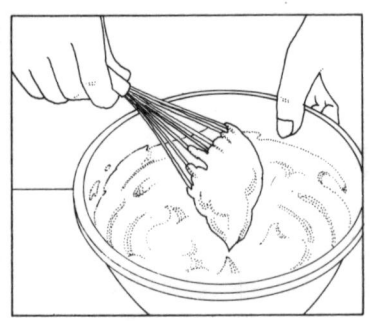

Whisking egg whites until stiff

pointed peaks when lifted from the eggs. Stiffly beaten egg whites should not fall out of the bowl if the bowl is upturned.

If using an electric beater, start on the lowest speed and gradually increase the speed. If the eggs are beaten too much the foam becomes dry and brittle and other ingredients such as sugar will not easily be incorporated.

FOLDING IN EGG WHITES

Mixtures combine more easily when their consistency and temperatures are similar. Folding in is best done with a metal spoon or plastic spatula. Use a continuous

Folding in with a metal spoon

cutting and lifting movement, scooping right down to the bottom of the bowl. Scoop one way turning the bowl the other. Stop folding as soon as the mixture is blended. Too much folding and the egg white may start to liquify.

Use leftover unbeaten egg whites for glazing pies, pastry and breads. Mix lightly with a pinch of salt and brush over rolls and breads.

- Use egg whites to make meringues or soufflés.

- Add a stiffly whisked egg white to whipped cream to make a lighter texture and to stretch the cream.

- Egg whites will keep in the refrigerator for 3-4 days. Cover tightly.

CUSTARD SAUCE
Makes $1\frac{1}{3}$ cups

2 eggs

2 tsp sugar

$1\frac{1}{3}$ cups milk

1 tsp vanilla extract (optional)

1 Beat the eggs with the sugar and 3 Tbsp milk. Heat the rest of the milk until warm and pour it slowly on to the eggs, beating all the time.

2 Pour into a double boiler or bowl standing over a pan of simmering water. Cook, stirring constantly, until the custard thickens enough to coat the back of a spoon.

3 Pour into a chilled bowl and stir in the vanilla extract. Serve warm or cold. The sauce thickens on cooling.

CRÈME PÂTISSIÈRE
Makes $1\frac{1}{3}$ cups

2 eggs

$\frac{1}{3}$ cup sugar

2 Tbsp all-purpose flour

2 Tbsp cornstarch

$1\frac{1}{3}$ cups milk

vanilla extract

1 Beat the eggs and sugar together until thick and pale in color. Stir the flour and cornstarch together and add a little cold milk to make a smooth paste. Add to egg mixture.

2 Heat the rest of the milk in a saucepan and stir over low heat until the mixture boils. Add egg mixture and a few drops of vanilla extract to taste to hot milk and cook for a further 2-3 minutes until thick and smooth. Cover and leave until cold before using as required.

MERINGUES

The light, crisp texture of meringues is the perfect foil to creamy fillings and slices of soft fruit. Meringues are made with whisked egg whites to which sugar is incorporated. They are very slowly baked in the oven in order to dry out and become crisp and firm. They are a perfect way to use up leftover egg whites because meringues will keep in an airtight container for as long as 6 weeks.

There are three basic types of meringue although for home cooking only meringue Suisse is usually made. Meringue *cuite* and Italian meringue are both made by cooking the egg whites and this enables the meringue to be stored if necessary before shaping. These meringues are harder, whiter and more powdery than meringue Suisse but require more painstaking care.

Meringue Suisse is made by incorporating sugar into stiffly beaten egg whites. First one half of the sugar is very gradually added, about 1 Tbsp at a time, while whisking after each addition until the sugar is fully incorporated and partially dissolved. Sugar added in large amounts at this stage may result in a cooked meringue which is sticky. The remaining sugar is added by sprinkling it over the whisked whites and folding it in with a metal spoon. The egg whites should be firm and glossy.

Meringue topping is made in the same way as meringue Suisse except that the amount of sugar is slightly decreased. Instead of using $\frac{1}{3}$ cup per 1 egg white, 4 Tbsp per egg white is used. The meringue is spread over the filling, which should be warm to help the meringue stick to it. It is baked at a higher temperature than other meringues to make its characteristic light spongy texture.

MERINGUE SUISSE

Makes about 15 individual meringue shapes

3 eggs whites
1 cup sugar

1 Grease a baking sheet or line it with aluminum foil or baking parchment.

2 Whisk the egg whites until stiff. Gradually add $\frac{1}{2}$ cup sugar, whisking well after each addition. Fold in the remaining sugar very lightly with a metal spoon.

3 Spoon the meringue into a pastry bag fitted with a large star nozzle and pipe small rounds on to the prepared baking sheet. Alternatively, spoon the mixture in small mounds on to the prepared baking sheet.

4 Bake in the oven at 250°F for about $2\frac{1}{2}$–3 hours, until firm and crisp, but still white. If they begin to brown, prop open the oven door a little. Remove the meringues from the baking sheet and leave until cold on a wire rack.

MERINGUE NESTS

Spoon the meringue into six mounds, spaced well apart on the prepared baking sheet; hollow out centers with the back of a spoon.

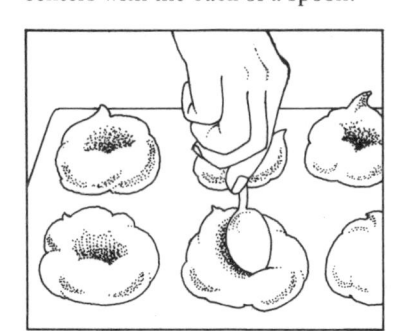

Hollowing out meringue nests

MERINGUE BASKET

Grease a 9-inch pie pan and spoon in the meringue. Pile the meringue high around the sides of the pan to make a basket.

MERINGUE SHELL

Draw an 8-inch circle on a sheet of baking parchment and place the paper mark side down on a baking sheet. Spread some of the meringue over the circle to form the base of the shell. Using a large star nozzle pipe the remainder to form the edge of the shell, or make a rim with the aid of a spoon. Bake for $1\frac{1}{2}$–2 hours.

PAVLOVA

3 egg whites
1 cup sugar
$\frac{1}{2}$ tsp vanilla extract
$\frac{1}{2}$ tsp white wine vinegar
1 tsp cornstarch
$1\frac{1}{3}$ cups cream
fresh strawberries, raspberries or kiwi fruit

1 Draw a 7-inch circle on baking parchment and place the paper mark side down on a baking sheet.

2 Whisk the egg whites until very stiff. Whisk in half the sugar, the extract, vinegar and cornstarch.

3 Spread the meringue mixture over the circle and bake in the oven at 300°F for about 1 hour until crisp and dry. Leave to cool on the baking sheet then carefully remove the paper.

4 Whisk the cream until stiff. Slide the meringue on to a flat plate, pile the cream on it and arrange the fruit on top.

SOUFFLÉS

Hot soufflés are based either on a sweet white sauce to which egg yolks and flavorings are added, or on a crème pâtissière, in which the egg yolks are already incorporated. Cold soufflés are usually based on fruit purées.

HOT VANILLA SOUFFLÉ

Serves 4–6

⅓ cup sugar
4 eggs, separated
4 Tbsp all-purpose flour
1¼ cups milk
½ tsp vanilla extract
confectioners sugar (optional)

1 Butter a 7 inch, 2-quart capacity soufflé dish. Cream the sugar with one whole egg and one yolk until pale cream in color. Stir in the flour. Pour on the milk and mix until smooth.

2 Pour the mixture into a saucepan and bring to boiling point, stirring, and simmer for 2 minutes. Cool slightly. Beat in remaining yolks and extract.

3 Whisk the egg whites until stiff then fold into the mixture. Pour into the prepared soufflé dish and bake in the oven at 350°F for about 45 minutes until well risen, firm to the touch and pale golden. Serve at once.

STRAWBERRY SOUFFLÉ

Serves 4–6

¾ lb strawberries
2 Tbsp powdered gelatine
4 Tbsp sugar
4 tsp lemon juice
3 egg whites
pinch of salt
¾ cup cream

1 Reserve six strawberries for decoration. Purée the remainder in a blender.

2 Put gelatine and 1 Tbsp sugar in a saucepan, add one third of purée and stir over gentle heat until gelatine dissolves.

3 Remove from the heat, stir in the remaining purée and the lemon juice and pour into a bowl. Chill until the mixture mounds slightly when dropped from spoon.

4 Prepare a paper collar (see page 48) for a 5-cup soufflé dish. Place dish on a baking sheet for easier handling.

5 Whisk egg whites and salt until soft peaks form. Add remaining sugar a little at a time, whisking well, until stiff peaks form.

6 Beat the chilled strawberry mixture in a mixer until fluffy. Whip cream until soft peaks form and combine with strawberry mixture. Carefully fold in egg whites.

7 Spoon soufflé mixture into dish and smooth the top. Chill for 4 hours until set. Peel off the collar from dish. Decorate with reserved strawberries.

CRÊPES

Crêpes are made with a batter of pouring consistency. Most batters will improve if they are left to rest in a cool place for at least 30 minutes before using; this will help make a lighter crêpe. If the crêpe mixture thickens after resting it can be thinned with a little milk. Crêpe batters made with a whisked egg white must be used straight away.

CRÊPES

Makes 8 crêpes

¾ cup all-purpose flour
pinch of salt
1 egg
1¼ cups milk
vegetable oil

1 Mix the flour and salt together, make a well in the center and break in the egg. Add half the liquid. Beat until smooth.

2 Add the remaining liquid gradually. Beat until the ingredients are well mixed.

3 Heat a little oil in a small frying pan running it around pan to coat sides. Raise handle side of pan slightly. Pour a little batter in from raised side, tilting pan to form an evenly round crêpe.

4 Place over a moderate heat and cook until golden underneath, then turn with a palette knife and cook the other side. Slide the crêpe on to a plate lined with wax paper. Repeat.

Pastry Making

Good pastry making is a knack which comes only from practice and an understanding of the ingredients and how they are combined. There are a number of types of pastries, each with their own special uses. All are worth knowing how to make if you want your desserts to have that extra home-made taste. Shortcrust pastry being the most commonly used, it is explained in detail on the following pages.

PASTRY

Flour, fat, and liquid are the main ingredients of pastry. The method in which the fat is incorporated into the flour as well as the proportion of fat to flour determines the different types of pastry.

Shortcrust pastry is the most popular pastry. Not only is it quick and easy to make, but its firm texture makes it ideal for pies and tarts. It uses half as much fat as flour. When making shortcrust pastry choose a fat which is firm at room temperature—it should be soft enough to cut into the flour yet firm enough so that the flour mixture does not mass into a lump. Butter gives the best flavor. Lard also gives a good flavor but is too soft at room temperature. For best results, use a combination of fats such as half lard and half solid vegetable shortening.

Rich shortcrust pastry is a variation of shortcrust pastry, made with beaten egg instead of water and with sugar added if a sweet flavor is required.

With *puff pastry* and other flaked pastries the proportion of fat to flour is much higher than with shortcrust pastries. They are the richest of all pastries, rising in golden flaky layers.

Strudel pastry or phyllo (filo) dough is a very crisp flaky pastry used for making strudels and Greek pastries. It must be made with bread flour to give the dough the elasticity it needs to be stretched until it is paper thin.

SHORTCRUST PASTRY

Good pastry making requires that you work quickly and handle the pastry as little as possible, otherwise the gluten in the flour will develop too much, resulting in an "overworked" dough and tough pastry. With such a high proportion of fat it is important that work conditions be cool. Work on a cool surface; and always use your fingertips, which are cooler than your palms.

Cutting is the way that fat is incorporated into flour when making shortcrust pastries. The fat is cut into small pieces with a pastry cutter or two knives.

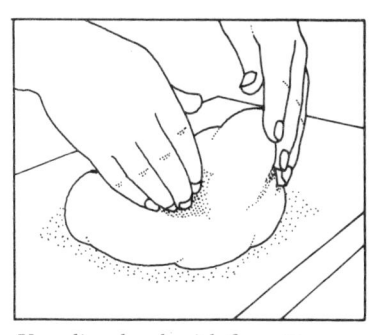

Kneading dough with fingertips

Kneading After liquid is added to the mixture to bind it, the dough should be gathered lightly together leaving the side of the bowl clean. Working on an unfloured surface, the dough is kneaded very lightly with the fingertips just long enough for it to be smooth and free from cracks.

Resting the dough Essential to all good pastry making is resting the dough to give the dough a chance to "relax," making it easier to roll out and also to help prevent shrinkage during baking. Always tightly wrap the dough in plastic wrap or foil. Refrigerate for 30 minutes.

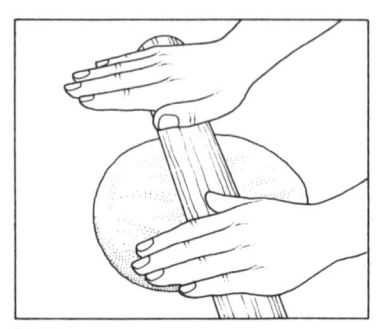

Rolling out pastry dough

Rolling out When rolling out pastry to the required shape and size never dust the pastry with flour. If necessary dust the working surface and rolling pin with as little flour as possible. With shortcrust pastry the dough can be rotated frequently to help create an even shape. Start by forming the dough roughly into the desired final shape and then roll away from you with short, quick rolls in one direction only. Rolled-out pastry should rest for 5 minutes before use.

SHAPING THE DOUGH
Avoid stretching the dough at any time otherwise it will only shrink when baked. It should also be handled as little as possible. Rolled-out pastry can be transferred to the dish to be lined by placing the rolling pin at one end of pastry and very loosely rolling the pastry around it, then unrolling it over the dish to be lined or covered. Alternatively, it can be folded in half and placed on one half of the dish and opened out to cover the whole dish.

FREEZING
Pastry dough should be shaped before freezing as thawing can take over 3 hours. Unbaked pie shells are very fragile. Foil plates or freezer proof ovenware should be used.

Freeze for up to 6 months.

BAKING A PIE SHELL
Having lined the pie pan with pastry, cut a piece of baking parchment or foil to act as a lining. Place it on the pastry and weigh it down with some dried beans, pasta, rice or ceramic baking beans. Bake pastry for 10–15 minutes, remove the weights and the lining and continue to cook the shell for a further 5 minutes.

Dried beans used for this method may be used many times. Pie shells so cooked will keep for a few days in an airtight container and can be frozen.

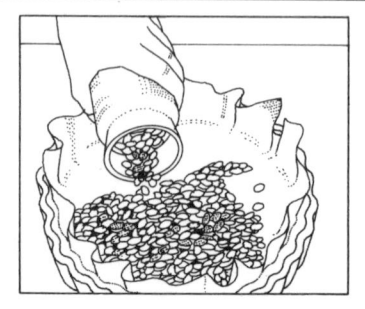

Pastry can be baked without defrosting but allow about 5 extra minutes cooking time.

Freeze uncooked fruit pies for up to 3 months; cooked fruit pies will keep for 6 months.

Bake uncooked fruit pies from frozen in a 425° oven for 40–60 minutes, according to type and size. Cooked pies should be thawed at room temperature for 2–4 hours, depending on type and size. Reheat, if necessary, in the oven.

QUANTITIES
Pastry amounts given in recipes are usually very generous to allow for slight variations in pan sizes. However, leftover trimmings can be used to make decorations.

FINISHING TOUCHES
Fluting or Scalloping Use a round bladed knife or table knife. Make a series of curves around the pie with the inward points $\frac{1}{2}$ inch inside the peaks of the flutes. Hold the pastry edge adjacent to where you are cutting.
Crimping With a thumb or finger of one hand push the pastry inward gently. With the finger of the other hand pinch the pastry pushed up initially. Continue around the edge of the pie.

PASTRY MAKING

PASTRY DECORATIONS
Pastry decorations should be stuck to the pie by brushing them with water or a beaten egg before arranging them on the surface.

Making pastry tassels

Tassels Cut a strip from the rolled out pastry trimming 1 inch wide and 4–6 inches long. Cut $\frac{3}{4}$-inch slits at short intervals to resemble a fringe. Roll up and stand on the uncut end while you spread out the cut strips to form the tassel.

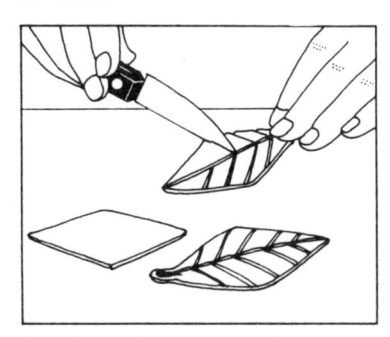

Marking veins on pastry leaves

Leaves Cut thinly rolled out pastry trimmings into 1-inch wide strips. Cut diagonally to diamond shapes and mark veins of a leaf on each one with back of a knife blade. Pinch one end to form a stem.

Shapes Use petits fours cutters and small round cutters to make different pastry shapes. Cut out fruit shapes or letters to denote the type of fruit in the pie.

Glazes Pies can be glazed with milk or beaten egg. Apply any glaze just before baking otherwise pastry may be soggy.

LINING A FLUTED TART PAN
Roll out the pastry thinly to a diameter approximately 2 inches wider all round than your pan. Rolling your pastry around the rolling pin lift it on to the pan and then when centered unroll the pin from the pastry. By lifting the edges of the pastry it will settle into the shape of the pan. Working away from the center with your fingertips gently press the pastry into place, taking special care to ensure the pastry fits into the "flutes." Make sure there are no air pockets between

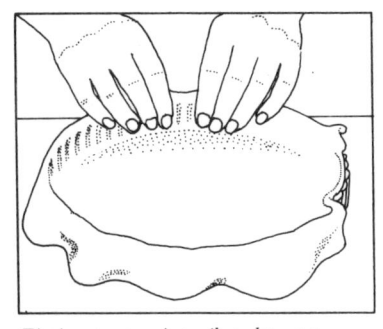

Fitting pastry into fluted tart pan

the pastry and the pan. You can now use a knife or scissors to trim the pastry, or, roll the excess pastry over the rim and run the rolling pin across the top for a neat trim.

LINING AND COVERING A DOUBLE CRUST PIE
Divide the dough into two, one part being slightly larger than the other. Shape both pieces into ball shapes ready for rolling. Start with the larger piece and roll it out until it is 1 inch wider than the rim of your pie pan. Transfer the pastry over the pan and allow it to settle into the shape. Taking care not to stretch the pastry, ease it to the shape of the pan making sure there are no air pockets. Put the pie filling, which should be cold, into the pastry-lined pan leaving a slightly raised contour in the middle. Roll out the smaller ball for the top crust about $\frac{1}{2}$ inch wider than the rim. Before transferring the pastry on to the pie, brush the rim with water. Seal the edge and glaze, making a short slit in center of pastry for the steam to escape.

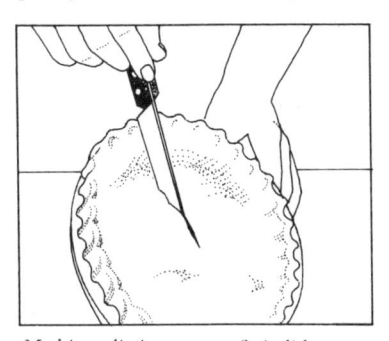

Making slit in center of pie lid

LINING SINGLE AND DOUBLE CRUST TARTS

Roll out the pastry and use a cutter $\frac{3}{4}$ inch larger than the

Piling the filling into tarts

hollow in your tartlet pan. If top crusts are required, use a cutter the same diameter as the hollows. Press the larger rounds into the hollows of the pans. Pile filling into a heap in the center of each tart. For a double crust tart brush the edges of the lids with water and place them wet side down over each tart. Press the edges of the lids on to the lower pastry linings to make a seal. Make a little incision in the top of each tart.

LINING SMALL TART PANS

Arrange the tart pans close together on a baking sheet. Roll out enough pastry to cover the area of pans. Transfer the pastry over the pans like a blanket. Twist off some of the pastry from around the edge and shape it into a ball

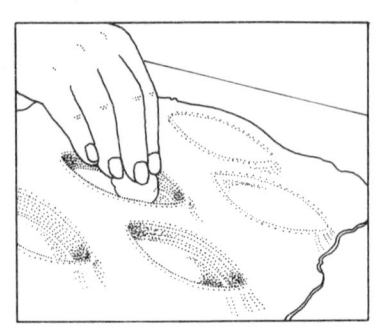

Easing pastry into small tart pans

and lightly flour it. Use this ball of pastry to ease the pastry into each pan making sure there are no air pockets below the pastry. Use the rolling pin to remove the excess pastry by pressing it down and running it across the top of the pans. Tidy the edges of the pans with your fingertips and prick base and sides with a fork.

SHORTCRUST PASTRY

| $1\frac{1}{2}$ cups all-purpose flour |
| pinch of salt |
| $\frac{1}{4}$ cup butter or margarine |
| $\frac{1}{4}$ cup lard |

1 Sift the flour and salt together in a bowl. Cut the butter and lard into small pieces and add to the flour.

2 Cut in the butter and the lard until the mixture resembles fine cornmeal.

3 Add 2–3 Tbsp chilled water evenly over the surface and stir in until the mixture begins to stick together in large lumps.

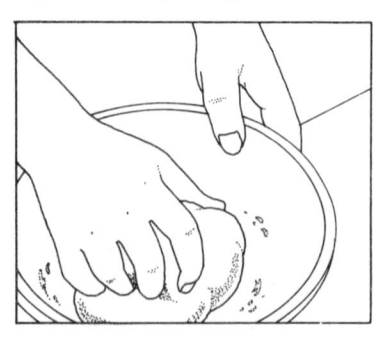

4 With one hand, collect the mixture together to form a ball. Knead lightly for a few seconds to give a firm, smooth dough. Do not over-handle.

5 The pastry can be used straight away, but it is better if allowed to "rest" for about 30 minutes wrapped in foil in the refrigerator.

6 Roll out the pastry on a lightly floured surface to a thickness about $\frac{1}{8}$ inch. Do not pull or stretch the pastry. To cook, the usual oven temperature is 400–425°F.

To freeze: Baked and unbaked shortcrust pastry freeze well. Thaw unrolled dough at room temperature before unwrapping; rolled out pastry may be cooked without defrosting allowing extra time to bake.

SPONGE SHELL

This is not strictly a pastry, but it is used in the same way as a baked pastry shell for cold fruit mixtures.

| melted shortening |
| 2 tsp and $\frac{1}{3}$ cup sugar |
| 1 tsp and $\frac{1}{3}$ cup all-purpose flour |
| 2 eggs |

1 Brush the inside of an 8-inch raised based flan pan with melted shortening. Leave until set then sprinkle over 2 tsp sugar and tilt the tin to coat evenly. Add 1 tsp flour and coat similarly, knocking out any excess.

2 Place the eggs and remaining sugar in a deep bowl and whisk vigorously, until the mixture is very thick. Sift remaining flour over the surface of the mixture. Fold gently through with a metal spoon, then turn into the prepared pan and tilt to level the surface.

3 Place on a baking sheet and bake in the oven at 350°F for 20–25 minutes. When cooked, the sponge will have shrunk away from the edges of the pan, be a light golden brown and will spring back when pressed lightly. Ease away from the edges of the sponge with the fingers and turn carefully on to a wire rack. Leave for 30 minutes until cool.

Sweet Sauces, Butters, Sugar and Gelatine

Sweet-flavored sauces and butters are quick and easy to make, and are an excellent way of livening up a dessert. Try them as accompaniments to steamed and baked puddings, cold soufflés and meringue desserts. Alternatively, sweet sauces are delicious simply poured over ice cream or fresh fruit. Sugar and sugar syrups are essential for many desserts. Here are ways to sweeten your desserts in new and classic ways. Gelatine is a dessert-maker's magic, but handling it requires understanding its properties. Use it confidently in these soufflés and molded desserts.

SWEET BUTTERS

BRANDY BUTTER
Makes 6–8 servings

| $\frac{1}{2}$ cup butter, softened |
| $1\frac{3}{4}$ cups confectioners sugar, sifted |
| $\frac{2}{3}$ cup sugar |
| 1 Tbsp milk |
| 1 Tbsp brandy |

1 Beat the butter until pale and light. Gradually beat in the sugars, alternately with the milk and brandy. Continue beating until light and fluffy. Pile into a small dish and leave to harden before serving.

──── VARIATIONS ────

Rum Butter Use brown sugar instead of granulated sugar, replace the brandy with 3 Tbsp rum and add the grated rind of $\frac{1}{2}$ a lemon and a squeeze of lemon juice.

Lemon or Orange Butter Omit the milk and brandy and add the grated rind and juice of 1 lemon or a small orange.

CHOCOLATE NUT BUTTER

| $\frac{1}{2}$ cup butter |
| 2 tsp sugar |
| 1 Tbsp grated semisweet chocolate |
| 2 Tbsp chopped walnuts |

1 Beat the butter until light and fluffy, then beat in the remaining ingredients.

SWEET SAUCES

SWEET WHITE SAUCE

| $1\frac{1}{2}$ Tbsp cornstarch |
| $1\frac{1}{3}$ cups milk |
| $1\frac{1}{2}$ Tbsp sugar |

1 Blend the cornstarch with 1–2 Tbsp of the milk to a smooth paste.

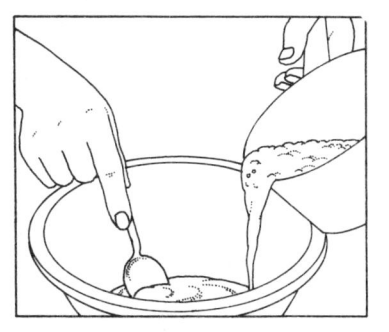

2 Heat the remaining milk until boiling and add to mixture, stirring. Return to pan and bring to the boil, stirring. Cook for 1–2 minutes after the mixture has thickened to a glossy sauce. Add sugar to taste.

──── VARIATIONS ────

When adding extra liquid to the sauce make a thicker sauce by increasing the quantity of cornstarch to 2 Tbsp.

Flavor with any of the following when sauce has thickened:
1 tsp allspice
2 Tbsp jam
grated rind of $\frac{1}{2}$ an orange or lemon
1–2 Tbsp rum
1 egg yolk (reheat but do not boil)

CHOCOLATE SAUCE
Makes about $1\frac{1}{3}$ cups

| 6 oz semisweet chocolate in pieces |
| 1 Tbsp butter |
| 3 Tbsp milk |
| 3 Tbsp light corn syrup |

1 Put the chocolate in a small bowl with the butter. Add the milk and syrup.

IRRESISTIBLE DESSERTS

2 Stand the bowl over a pan of warm water and heat gently, stirring, until the chocolate has melted and the sauce is warm.

FUDGE SAUCE

Makes about 2 cups
| 2 oz semisweet chocolate |
| 2 Tbsp butter |
| 4 Tbsp warm milk |
| 1½ cups brown sugar |
| 2 Tbsp light corn syrup |
| 1 tsp vanilla extract |

1 Break up the chocolate and put into a bowl standing over a saucepan of hot water. Add the butter. Leave until the chocolate and butter have melted, stirring once or twice.

2 Off the heat, blend in the milk and transfer the chocolate mixture to a saucepan. Add sugar and syrup.

3 Stir over a low heat until the sugar has dissolved. Bring to the boil and boil steadily without stirring for 5 minutes. Remove pan from heat. Add vanilla extract and mix well. Serve hot with ice cream, and steamed puddings.

BUTTERSCOTCH NUT SAUCE

Makes about ½ cup
| 2 Tbsp butter |
| 2 Tbsp brown sugar |
| 1 Tbsp light corn syrup |
| 3 Tbsp chopped nuts |
| squeeze of lemon juice (optional) |

1 Warm the butter, sugar, and syrup in a saucepan until well blended. Boil for 1 minute and stir in the nuts and lemon juice.

JAM SAUCE

Makes about 1 cup
| 4 Tbsp jam, seeds removed |
| ⅔ cup juice, drained from a can of fruit |
| 2 tsp arrowroot |
| 2 Tbsp cold water |
| squeeze of lemon juice, optional |

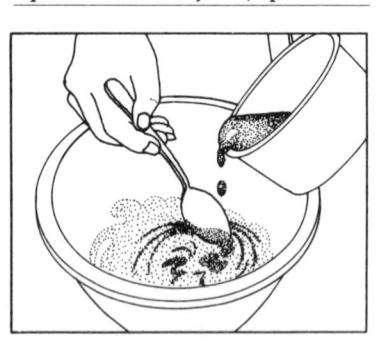

1 Warm the jam with the fruit juice and simmer gently for 5 minutes, stirring to blend well. Blend the arrowroot and cold water to a smooth cream and stir in the jam mixture.

2 Return to the pan and heat gently until it thickens and clears, stirring constantly. Add the lemon juice.

———— VARIATION ————

Thick jam sauce Omit the fruit juice and arrowroot. Heat the jam gently in a heavy-based saucepan until just melted and stir in a little lemon juice.

LEMON SAUCE

Makes about 1½ cups
| juice and grated rind of 1 large lemon |
| 1 Tbsp cornstarch |
| 2 Tbsp sugar |
| 1 Tbsp butter |
| 1 egg yolk, optional |

1 Add enough water to the lemon juice to measure 1⅓ cups. Add the lemon rind. Blend a little of the liquid with the cornstarch and the sugar until smooth.

2 Bring the remaining liquid to the boil and stir into the creamed cornstarch. Return all the liquid to the pan and bring to the boil, stirring until the sauce thickens and clears. Add butter.

3 Cool, beat in the egg yolk if used and reheat without boiling, stirring all the time.

———— VARIATION ————

Orange sauce Use the juice and rind of an orange instead of a lemon.

154

SWEET SAUCES, BUTTERS, SUGAR AND GELATINE

CINNAMON CREAM SAUCE

Makes ⅔ cup

⅔ cup light cream
1 tsp sugar
¼ tsp ground cinnamon

Pour the cream into a bowl, stir in the sugar and cinnamon until evenly blended, then chill.

HOT SABAYON SAUCE

Makes about ⅔ cup

2 egg yolks
⅓ cup sugar
pinch of arrowroot
½ cup sherry or white wine

1 Beat the egg yolks and sugar together until pale and creamy. Blend the arrowroot with the sherry or white wine and gradually whisk this into the egg and sugar mixture. Place the bowl over a pan of gently simmering water and whisk until thick and frothy. Serve at once.

COLD SABAYON SAUCE

Makes about ⅔ cup

⅓ cup sugar
4 Tbsp water
2 egg yolks, beaten
grated rind of ½ a lemon
juice of 1 lemon
2 Tbsp rum or sherry
2 Tbsp light cream

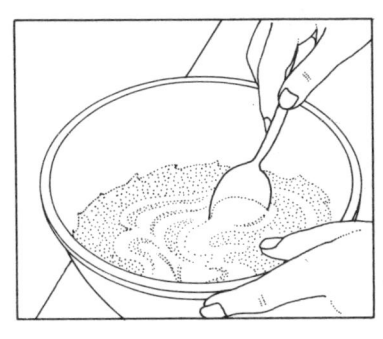

1 Dissolve the sugar in the water and boil for 2–3 minutes, until syrupy. Pour slowly on to the yolks whisking until pale and thick. Add the lemon rind, lemon juice and rum or sherry and whisk for a further few minutes. Fold in the cream and chill well.

MOUSSELINE SAUCE

Makes about ⅔ cup

1 egg
1 egg yolk
3 Tbsp sugar
1 Tbsp sherry
4 Tbsp light cream

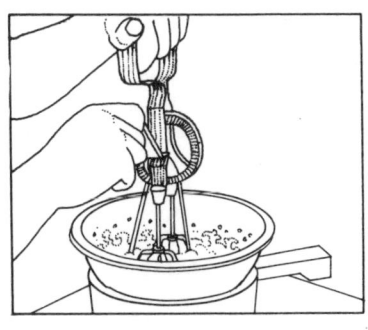

1 Place all the ingredients in a bowl over a pan of boiling water and whisk until pale and frothy and of a creamy thick consistency. Serve at once.

COFFEE CREAM SAUCE

Makes about ¾ cup

2 tsp instant coffee powder
⅔ cup cream
1 Tbsp milk
2 Tbsp sugar
vanilla extract

1 Dissolve the coffee powder in 2 tsp hot water. Cool slightly and mix in the cream, milk, sugar and a few drops of vanilla extract. Whisk until the cream begins to hold its shape.

Sugar

Desserts depend on sugars for their sweetening power, and they also give many desserts their characteristic textures and consistencies as well as color—the smooth syrupy consistency of many sauces, the soft spongy texture of cakes, the crispness of meringues and the rich color of some steamed puddings. When using sugar be careful about altering the amount called for in the recipe: too little sugar or too much and the texture of your dessert may be spoiled. Remember sugar tastes much sweeter when desserts are served hot—so less sugar is needed. Conversely, cold puddings require more sugar and will taste almost too sweet before they have cooled.

Granulated sugar is most frequently used in dessert making. In dessert recipes it is called for simply as "sugar."

The powdery fine texture of *confectioners sugar* makes it ideal for using with uncooked fruit purées which are used for making sorbets or sauces—it quickly dissolves without heat. Confectioners sugar is used for making icings and also makes a simple and attractive topping when lightly sifted over cakes, pies and pastries. Do not use it for baking as the volume produced will be dense and heavy.

Brown sugars can all be creamed easily with butter. Unlike white sugar brown sugar not only sweetens but adds flavor as well, especially dark brown sugar which adds a dark color to many steamed dried fruit puddings and fruit cakes.

Liquid sweeteners
Honey makes a lovely dessert topping. It absorbs and retains moisture and helps prevent cakes from drying out and going stale. Only part of the sugar content should be replaced by honey—usually not more than half—otherwise the texture will be altered. When honey is used to make ice creams they will have a softer consistency.

Molasses adds dark color and a distinctive, flavor to desserts.

TO MEASURE HONEY
To measure with a measuring spoon, first warm spoon under hot water—scooping the sweetener will be easier.

Sugar Syrups

Sugar syrups form the basis of a number of simple fruit desserts and they are also used when making bottled fruits and for freezing fruits. Sugar syrups vary in the amount of sugar which is dissolved in water: they can be light, medium or heavy. Which one you make depends on the intended use or on the type of fruit.

Although these syrups are boiled they are only boiled for 1 minute—quite unlike the lengthy boiling of syrups made for use in candy making.

When making a simple sugar syrup the sugar must first be slowly dissolved over gentle heat before it is brought to the boil, otherwise when cooled the syrup may crystallize. The sugar is then boiled for 1 minute. To cut the time for the syrup to cool dissolve the sugar in half the water, bring the water to the boil for 1 minute, then add the remaining water. If the syrup is to be used while still boiling, keep the lid on the pan to prevent evaporation, which would alter the strength of the syrup.
To make a light sugar syrup use $1\frac{1}{3}$ cups sugar for $2\frac{2}{3}$ cups water.

This syrup is used when making fresh fruit salads, for poaching fruits and in freezing fruits like fresh dates and figs, slices of lemon and lime and rhubarb and pineapple.

To make a medium sugar syrup use 2 cups sugar for 2⅔ cups water.
This syrup is used for soaking savarins and rum babas and for freezing fruit like apples, oranges, apricots, peaches, and plums.
To make heavy sugar syrup use 2⅔ cups for every 2⅔ cups water.
Use for bottling and freezing fruit such as most tart soft berry fruits.

POACHED OR STEWED FRUITS IN SUGAR SYRUP

Fresh fruits lightly cooked in a flavored sugar syrup make a simple yet elegant dessert, especially when served with cream or

Turning fruit during poaching

custard sauce. Use firm fruits as soft fruits will not hold their shape easily. When cooking fruits use a heavy-based pan large enough for the fruit to stand in one layer so that it cooks evenly. Turn the fruit occasionally with a slotted spoon.
For every 1 lb fruit use 2⅔ cups light sugar syrup. The fruit should be very gently simmered in the sugar syrup until it is almost cooked — usually this takes about 5–7 minutes. To prevent the fruit from becoming mushy remove the pan from the heat and leave the fruit in the pan, covered, for several more minutes while it finishes cooking.

FLAVORINGS FOR 1 lb POACHED FRUIT

Apples Add a squeeze of lemon juice, a strip of lemon rind, 1 or 2 cloves or a small piece of cinnamon stick.
Peaches Add 3–4 Tbsp brandy after the fruit has cooked.
Pears Add 1 or 2 cloves or a piece of cinnamon stick.
Rhubarb Add a piece of ginger root, a piece of cinnamon stick or, alternatively, a strip of lemon or orange rind.

CARAMEL SUGAR

To make caramel sugar, sugar is cooked until it turns a brown color. The caramel can range from straw-colored to a deep brown; this depends on how long the sugar is cooked. Caramel sugar tastes much less sweet than ordinary sugar and has a distinctive flavor.

To make a hard caramel, the browned sugar is poured on to a lightly oiled baking tray and left until brittle and hard. It can then be broken into pieces or crushed to a powder with a rolling pin. Use sprinkled on puddings in the same way as praline.

Caramel sugar can also be thinned with water to make a syrup for crème caramel or caramelized oranges. Be very careful when adding water to the hot

Sprinkling pieces of hard caramel

sugar — it will spurt and bubble. Remove the pan from the heat and add the water very slowly. If the syrup is too thin, it can be boiled until reduced to the desired thickness. A caramel syrup can also be made by first dissolving the sugar in the water over low heat and then boiling until the syrup turns the desired shade of brown.

TO COAT A DISH WITH CARAMEL

The dish to be coated with caramel should be warmed to enable the caramel to slide more easily over it. If using a metal dish, use hot pads or hold the dish in a cloth as the hot caramel quickly heats the dish. Tilt the

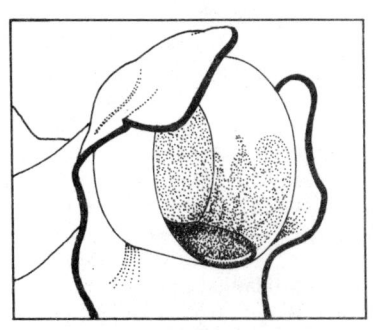

Coating a dish with caramel

dish gently until it is evenly coated. Allow the caramel to cool slightly before adding custard.

FLAVORED SUGARS

Bay leaf Store sugar with 1–2 bay leaves in a tightly closed airtight container. Use the sugar for making puddings.
Lemon or orange Mix ⅔ cup sugar with the finely grated rind of 1 lemon or orange. Leave the sugar to dry then store in a tightly covered airtight container.
Vanilla Store 1 whole vanilla bean in a tightly closed airtight container of sugar.

Gelatine

Gelatine is a tasteless substance which when chilled gives fruit, pudding and mousses their special wobbly and soothing consistency.

Powdered gelatine is sold loose in cartons or in measured envelopes, each containing exactly 0.4 oz gelatine which is the equivalent of 1 Tbsp. This amount of gelatine will set $2\frac{1}{4}$ cups of liquid. If too much gelatine is used the finished dessert will be stiff or rubbery. However, sometimes about 1–2 Tbsp extra gelatine is added if the dish is to be served during hot weather or if the mixture is very acidic. To use powdered gelatine, always add the gelatine to the liquid. Place a small amount of cold recipe liquid in a heatproof cup or bowl and sprinkle in the gelatine. Stand the bowl over a saucepan of hot water and heat gently until the gelatine has dissolved. Use 3 Tbsp recipe liquid for each 1 Tbsp powdered gelatine. The gelatine must not be allowed to boil as boiling prevents proper setting from taking place.

When making *fruit gelatines*, warm the required amount of liquid, sweeten and flavor it, then quickly stir in the dissolved gelatine. The more closely the two are the same temperature the more easily the gelatine can be evenly blended with the liquid.

To hasten the set, heat one-half of the liquid, add the gelatine then combine with the remaining cold liquid. Gelatines will also set more quickly if the mixture is put into small molds or individual containers.

For mousses and other cold mixtures a little of the cold mixture should be added to the hot dissolved gelatine, then, holding the bowl high above the mixture pour it in a thin steady stream on to the cold mixture, whisking all the time so that the gelatine is completely blended.

Chilling takes up to 4 hours but longer if it contains fruit. For a firm set allow 12 hours.

TO UNMOLD A GELATINE DESSERT OR MOUSSE

Draw the tip of a knife or your finger around the rim of the mold to loosen the edge of the Jello. Immerse the mold in hot water for 2–3 seconds and place a wetted

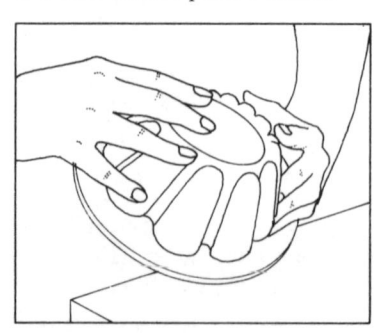

Unmolding Jello on to a plate

serving plate on top of the mold. Hold in position with both hands then quickly invert together giving one or two sharp shakes. If the mold is not positioned in the center, the wetted plate will make moving it into position easier.

TO SET FRUIT IN GELATINE

Fresh pineapple juice, pineapple and kiwi fruit contain an enzyme which breaks down gelatine and destroys its setting powers. Boil pineapple juice for 2–3 minutes to kill the enzyme. Do not use fresh or frozen pineapple or kiwi fruit.

Prepare a variety of fresh fruits such a grapes, bananas, sections of oranges and raspberries. Pour about 1 inch lemon Jello into a mold and arrange a little of the fruit in this. Allow the Jello to set. Add more Jello and fruit and allow to set. Continue until mold is filled.

INDEX

Almonds 141:
   To grind almonds 142
   To split almonds 141
Angelica leaves, to make 140
Apples 132:
   Apple almond checkerboard 70
   Apple and banana fritters 94
   Danish "peasant girl in a veil" 74
   Old-Fashioned apple pie 9
   Spiced apple and plum crumble 65
   Tarte française 16
   Tarte tatin 108
Apricots 132:
   Apricot glaze 139
   Brandied stuffed apricots 118
   Marbled apricot soufflé 48

Baked Alaska 28
Baked cherries 108
Bakewell pudding 61
Baking dishes 131
Bananas 132:
   Apple and banana fritters 94
   Banana chartreuse 53
   Banana cheesecake 42
   Crêpes creole 87
   Meringue basket 56
   Pineapple and banana flambé 120
Batter for crêpes 148
Bay leaf sugar 157
Blackberries 132-3
   Blackberry and pear cobbler 69
Blueberry sauce 139
Bombe mold 131
Brandied cherry sauce 139
Brandied stuffed apricots 118
Brandy butter 153
Brandy creams, frozen 100
Brazilnuts 141
Brown sugar 156
Butterscotch cream pie 20
Butterscotch nut sauce 154

Candied peel 140
Cape gooseberries 137
Caramel, to coat a dish with 157
Caraque 144
Cashew nuts 141
Charlotte mold 130
Charlotte russe 37
Cheesecake:
   Banana cheesecake 42
Cherries 133:
   Baked cherries 108
   Brandied cherry sauce 139
   Cherry strudel 22-3
   Snowcap iced pudding 34
Chilled zabaglione 33
China mold 131
Chinese lantern 137

Chocolate 143-4
   To decorate with chocolate 143-4
   To melt chocolate 143
   Chocolate nut butter 153
   Chocolate sauce 153
   Hot chocolate soufflé 47
   Magic chocolate pudding 77
   Nègre en chemise 32
   Petits pots au chocolat 31
   Profiteroles 44
Choux pastry 44
Christmas plum pudding 79
Cinnamon cream sauce 155
Citrus soufflé 116
Clementines 137
Coconuts, to prepare, shred and toast 142
Coffee:
   Coffee cream sauce 155
   Coffee-nut ice cream 41
   Rum and coffee pudding 95
Confectioners custard 146
Confectioners sugar 156
Copper bowl 130
Cottage cheese tart 73
Cream 144
Creamy plum sauce 139
Crema fritta 96
Crème brûlée 86
Crème caramel 85
Crème pâtissière 146
Crêpes Suzette 27
Crystallized fruits 140
Crystallized violets and roses 140
Currant roll 83
Currants 133
Custard pots 131
Custard sauce 146

Damsons 137
Danish "peasant girl in a veil" 74
Dried fruits 140-1

Eggs:
   To cook with eggs 145-6
   To separate an egg 145
   Egg whites 145-6
English trifle 59
Equipment 130-1

Figs 138
Floating islands 91
Fritters:
   Apple and banana fritters 94
Frozen desserts. See also Ice creams
   Chilled zabaglione 33
   Frozen brandy creams 100
   Snowcap iced pudding 34
Fruit. See also Apple, Apricot, etc
   To poach or stew fruits in syrup 157
   To set fruit in gelatine 158
   Dried fruits 140-1
   Flavorings for poached fruit 157
   Frudités 125

Fruit glazes 139
Fruit purées 139
Fruit sauces 138-9
Fruit spongecakes 6
List of fruits 132-8
Unusual fruits 136
Fudge nut pie 24
Fudge sauce 154

Gelatine 158
   To set fruit in gelatine 158
   To unmold a gelatine 158
Glacé cherries 140
Glace fruits 140; to remove sugary coating from 141
Glazes, fruit 139
Gooseberries 133
Granulated sugar 156
Grapefruit 133
Grapes 133
Guavas 138

Hazelnuts 141:
   To chop or grind hazelnuts 142
   To skin hazelnuts 142
   Coffee-nut ice cream 41
Honey 156; to measure 156

Ice creams and sorbets 144:
   Coffee-nut ice cream 41
   Kiwi fruit sorbet 123
   Praline ice cream 99
   Raspberry parfait 122
   Tutti frutti ice cream 105

Jam sauce 154
Jelly roll with hot jam sauce 82

Kiwi fruit 133
   Kiwi fruit sorbet 123
Kumquats 134

Lemon surprise 80
Lemons 134:
   Lemon butter 153
   Lemon sauce 154
   Lemon sugar 157
Limes 134:
   Lime meringue pie 60
Lychees 138
   Mandarin and lychee mousse 126

Macadamia nuts 141
Magic chocolate pudding 77
Mandarin and lychee mousse 126
Mangoes 134
Marbled apricot soufflé 48
Melba sauce 139
Melons 134-5:
   To make melon balls 135
   To make a melon basket 135
   To serve round melons 134
   Types of melon 134
Meringues 147
Meringue basket 56; to make 147
Meringue nests 147

Meringue shell 147
Meringue Suisse 147
Meringue surprise framboise 50
Mincemeat meringue tartlets 13
Molasses 156
Molds 130-1
Mousse:
   To unmold a mousse 158
   Mandarin and lychee mousse 126
Mousseline sauce 155

Nectarines 135
Nègre en chemise 32
Noodle pudding 71
Nuts 141-2. See also Almonds etc.
   To blanch nuts 141
   To chop or grind nuts 142
   To toast and roast nuts 142
   Butterscotch nut sauce 154
   Fudge nut pie 24

Old-Fashioned apple pie 9
Old-Fashioned maple pie 62
Oranges 135:
   Crêpes Suzette 27
   Orange butter 153
   Orange sugar 157
   Oranges in caramel 117
   Oranges en surprise 45
   Rhubarb and orange chiffon pie 111

Papayas 138
Passion fruit 138
Pastries. See also Pies, Tarts
   Cherry strudel 22-3
   Pears en chemise 18
Pastry:
   To bake a pie shell 150
   Choux pastry 44
   Finishing touches with pastry 150
   Freezing pastry 150
   Lining and covering a double crust pie 151
   Lining a fluted tart pan 151
   Lining single and double tarts 152
   Pastry decorations 151
   Pastry making techniques 149-50
   Shortcrust pastry 152
Pavlova 147
Peaches 135:
   Peach pie 10
Peanuts 141; to skin 142
Pears 135:
   Blackberry and pear cobbler 69
   Pears en chemise 18
   Poires Belle Hélène 115
Pecan nuts 141; to chop 142
Persimmons 138
Petits pots au chocolat 31
Pie pans 131
Pies. See also Tarts
   Butterscotch cream pie 20

159

IRRESISTIBLE DESSERTS

Fudge-nut pie 24
Lime meringue pie 60
Old-Fashioned apple pie 9
Old-Fashioned maple pie 62
Peach pie 10
Pumpkin pie 11
Rhubarb and orange chiffon pie 111
Rich chocolate pie 66
Pineapples 136
  Meringue basket 56
  Pineapple and banana flambé 120
Pistachio nuts 141
Plums 136
  Creamy plum sauce 139
  Spiced apple and plum crumble 65
Poires Belle Hélène 115
Pomegranates 136
Praline 141; to make 142
Praline ice cream 99
Pressure cooked puddings 131
Prickly pears 138
Profiteroles 44
Prune and port cream 128
Pudding molds 130
Puddings:
  To pressure cook puddings 131
  To steam puddings 131
  Apple-almond checkerboard 70
  Blackberry and pear cobbler 69

Christmas plum pudding 79
Currant roll 83
Jelly roll with hot jam sauce 82
Lemon surprise 80
Magic chocolate pudding 77
Noodle pudding 71
Rum and coffee pudding 95
Snowcap iced pudding 34
Spiced apple and plum crumble 65
Pumpkin pie 11

Quinces 136

Ramekins 131
Raspberries 136:
  Baked Alaska 28
  Melba Sauce 139
  Raspberry cream, crunchy 72
  Raspberry parfait 122
  Raspberry walnut torte 54–5
  Rødgrød 112
Red currant:
  Red currant glaze 139
  Rødgrød 112
Rhubarb 137:
  Rhubarb and orange chiffon pie 111
Rødgrød 112
Rum butter 153
Rum and coffee pudding 95
Rum soufflé omelette 88

Sabayon sauce 155; cold 155

Sauces:
Blueberry sauce 139
Brandied cherry sauce 139
Butterscotch nut sauce 154
Chocolate sauce 153
Cinnamon cream sauce 155
Coffee cream sauce 155
Creamy plum sauce 139
Custard sauce 146
Fruit sauce 138
Fudge sauce 154
Jam sauce 154
Lemon sauce 154
Melba sauce 139
Mousseline sauce 155
Sabayon sauce, hot or cold 155
Strawberry sauce 139
Sweet white sauce 153
Shortcrust pastry 152
Snowcap iced pudding 34
Sorbets *see* Ice creams and sorbets
Soufflé dish 131
Soufflé omelette:
  Rum soufflé omelette 88
Soufflés:
  Citrus soufflé 116
  Hot chocolate soufflé 47
  Hot vanilla soufflé 148
  Marbled apricot soufflé 48
  Strawberry soufflé 148
Spiced apple and plum crumble 65
Sponge shell 152

Strawberries 137
  Strawberry custard tart 14
  Strawberry sauce 139
  Strawberry soufflé 138
Strudel pastry 149
Sugar syrups 156–7
Sugar, types of 156
Sweet butters 153

Tangerines 137
Tartlet molds 131
Tarts. *See also* Pies:
  To line cases with pastry 151–2
  Bakewell pudding 61
  Mincemeat meringue tartlets 13
  Strawberry custard tarts 14
  Tarte Française 16
  Tarte Tatin 108
  Walnut meringue tart 15
Tea cream 102
Tipsy cake 38
Trifle, English 59
Tutti frutti ice cream 105

Vanilla soufflé, hot 148
Vanilla sugar 157

Walnuts 141:
  To chop walnuts 142
  Chocolate nut butter 153
  Raspberry walnut torte 54–5
Walnut meringue tart 15
White sauce, sweet 153

Zabaglione, chilled 33